A. C. Bradley on
Shakespeare's Tragedies

Y0-AGK-233

Related Palgrave Macmillan titles
Shakespearean Tragedy, 4th Edition by A. C. Bradley, with a new
   introduction by Robert Shaughnessy

Other books by John Russell Brown
Shakespeare and his Comedies
Free Shakespeare
Theatre Language
Shakespeare: Writing for Performance
What is Theatre?
New Sites for Shakespeare: Theatre, the Audience and Asia
Shakespeare: The Tragedies
Shakespeare and the Theatrical Event
Shakespeare Dancing
Macbeth (The Shakespeare Handbooks)
Hamlet (The Shakespeare Handbooks)
The Oxford Illustrated History of Theatre (editor)

A. C. Bradley on Shakespeare's Tragedies

A Concise Edition and Reassessment

JOHN RUSSELL BROWN

palgrave
macmillan

Introduction, selection and editorial matter © John Russell Brown 2007

All rights reserved. No reproduction, copy or transmission of
this publication may be made without written permission.

No paragraph of this publication may be reproduced, copied or
transmitted save with written permission or in accordance with
the provisions of the Copyright, Designs and Patents Act 1988,
or under the terms of any licence permitting limited copying
issued by the Copyright Licensing Agency, 90 Tottenham Court Road,
London W1T 4LP.

Any person who does any unauthorized act in relation to this
publication may be liable to criminal prosecution and civil
claims for damages.

The author has asserted his right to be identified as the author
of this work in accordance with the Copyright, Designs and
Patents Act 1988.

First published 2007 by
PALGRAVE MACMILLAN
Houndmills, Basingstoke, Hampshire RG21 6XS and
175 Fifth Avenue, New York, N.Y. 10010
Companies and representatives throughout the world

PALGRAVE MACMILLAN is the global academic imprint of the Palgrave
Macmillan division of St. Martin's Press, LLC and of Palgrave Macmillan Ltd.
Macmillan® is a registered trademark in the United States, United
Kingdom and other countries. Palgrave is a registered trademark in the
European Union and other countries.

ISBN-13: 978–0–230–00755–0
ISBN-10: 0–230–00755–4

This book is printed on paper suitable for recycling and
made from fully managed and sustained forest sources.

A catalogue record for this book is available from the British Library.

A catalog record for this book is available from the Library of Congress.

10   9   8   7   6   5   4   3   2   1
16   15   14   13   12   11   10   09   08   07

Printed and bound in China

Contents

Preface

The text of *Shakespearean Tragedy*, and page references to it, are taken from the fourth edition of 2006. Bradley's lecture on *Antony and Cleopatra* is quoted from *Oxford Lectures on Poetry* (London: Macmillan, 2nd edition, 1909), that on *Coriolanus* from *A Miscellany* (London: Macmillan, 1929). Minor changes in punctuation, capitalization, paragraphing, and the numbering of statements or arguments are introduced without comment for the sake of clarity or to avoid unnecessary complications. Editorial additions are printed within square brackets and omissions in the course of a passage are marked by a number of ellipses or, in some cases, a space and three asterisks. Only a few of Bradley's footnotes are retained.

Quotations from Shakespeare in *Shakespearean Tragedy* are from the Globe edition, the text that Bradley used throughout his book. Editorial quotations are from the edition by Peter Alexander (London: Collins, 1951, and many times reprinted).

While preparing this book I have consulted on numerous occasions with Robert Shaughnessy who, in preparation for his Introduction to the fourth and full edition of *Shakespearean Tragedy*, was exploring the cultural and scholarly contexts in which Bradley had written. He was both my critic and support in a most collaborative and friendly spirit: I am much in his debt and glad to be so.

At Palgrave Macmillan I could always count on Kate Wallis to further the project and supply advice on the needs of both publisher and readers. As the copy went to press, Valery Rose and Jocelyn Stockley have been assiduous and helpful in every possible way. I know how fortunate I have been to benefit from their skills; I am most grateful and my book much better prepared for its readers.

April 2006   **John Russell Brown**

Introduction

Some students take readily to A. C. Bradley's *Shakespearean Tragedy*, written more than a hundred years ago, and set about reading its sequence of lectures and copious notes in one long, private session. They are likely to be the same readers who enjoy the long novels with a moral purpose that, like Bradley's criticism, were written as the nineteenth century was coming to its end. Both forms of writing were in keeping with major elements in the culture of that time and Bradley's fame was soon established; it is more surprising that it has lasted so strongly to the present day.

Everyone with more than a passing interest in Shakespeare will have encountered his name and many without knowing why he achieved such prominence in the study of Shakespeare. This book sets out to explain his achievement, offer a concise edition of the lengthy original, and defend Bradley from much harsh criticism and occasional ridicule that his work has attracted over the years.

Shakespearean Tragedy does not immediately grip attention and positively encourage readers to read on. The first two chapters on the 'substance' and 'construction' of the plays are packed so full with brief references to all the tragedies, both early and late, and to the comedies and histories, that a reader not already well acquainted with Shakespeare's complete works will be unable to follow the argument closely and consistently. Even browsing through the later chapters on single plays is likely to prove difficult because Bradley did not write in a style that is used today and lacked the sharp rigour of the best contemporary criticism. Throughout we are likely to stumble at his recurrent use of *spiritual*, *soul*, *moral order*, *superior power*, *sweetness of spirit*, and other very general concepts.

When I was an undergraduate and wanted to know what this apparently unsinkable critic had to say, I read no more than a few pages before I lost patience and put the book down. I tried again later, after I had started to publish about Shakespeare on my own account, but it was still some years before I had read Bradley's every word and began to benefit directly from his truly amazing and unprecedented enterprise. For students who are experiencing a similar resistance to his writing and for readers with limited time who are drawn to the inner psychological tensions and uncertainties of Shakespeare's plays, this concise version offers a more welcoming entrance to his criticism than the full text of *Shakespearean Tragedy* and argues that it is a useful and even necessary part of our understanding of the tragedies. I doubt if anyone today would want to imitate Bradley's style of writing or be content with all his conclusions but by assimilating his methods of study we can strengthen our grasp of the plays and find that his insights quicken our own responses. I hope to present enough of his book in accessible form to encourage readers to study the plays for themselves with a patience and imagination similar to Bradley's, and to do so in their own ways and for their own purposes.

Part I analyses Bradley's critical and scholarly methods and examines his claim to permanent value for a study of the tragedies. On more general grounds, they are shown to be relevant to the study of all script-based drama. What he called an 'eager mind' or 'a vivid and intent imagination' (p. xlvii) enabled Bradley to envisage and then analyse what happens when written dialogue becomes the basis for performance and, in this process, changes in effect and gathers meanings that are as eloquent as they are transitory. He did not write about specific productions or performances but frequent theatre-going helped him to enact the plays over and over again in his mind and in such a palpable way that his senses and emotions were awakened, as well as his intellect, and raised questions that demanded answers. He asks readers to study a play as if they were actors who had to act 'all the parts' (p. xlvii). As its action unfolds in the reader's mind, the persons of the play will take on a local form and inhabit a particular place as if they were embodied in an actor's presence and had become actually alive. This form of actor-centred and yet imaginary performance can easily become self-indulgent and overly subtle or sentimental but Bradley, by using his copious and precise memory of the texts, was persistently sceptical and seemingly tireless in exploration. He continually criticized his own conclusions and carefully honed the drama as it was enacted in his mind. In this private and personal endeavour, he had much in common with leading actors of his day, Henry Irving and Ellen Terry outstandingly, among others; their writings and interviews are lasting testimonies to a constant questioning of the texts and their own responses. In his thinking about the inner consciousness of individual characters Bradley also had affinities with Stanislavski and Freud, two contemporaries whose writings and ideas were unknown to him.

Such an engagement with the texts has permanent value for any study of drama that respects a play's theatricality and seeks out its potential in performance. Unlike much current 'performance criticism', Bradley's understanding was not limited by the achievements of individual actors and productions or by the theatrical fashions of his time and place. He was endlessly resourceful, responding to hesitations and uncertainties as well as clear verbal statements or irreversible actions. He was aware of the temporary and unstable nature of any theatrical event, the progressive nature of a performance, and an audience's changing expectations as the narrative advances.

Having lectured and taught in large and small classes in both universities and adult classes, in Liverpool, Glasgow and Oxford, Bradley had a strong sense of his readers as audiences. He was able to engage them in argument and lead them by degrees ever deeper into the texts and the possible meanings that lie within them. At the same time he would draw on earlier literature and entertain judgements that were not his own. His book offers a progressive understanding of the plays that is still effective today, once the unfamiliar elements in his language – its generalized concepts and, perhaps above all, its tempo and rhythm – are no longer felt as deterrents but accepted as his vehicle for thoughtful and, at times, adventurous discourse. This critic lets us know when he is taking risks and stands back for us to follow if we wish or if we can. Gradually we gain confidence in our guide, even if we cannot entirely share in his quest. The first part of this book is intended to assist in this process and make the journey more enjoyable by noting the advantages and limitations of this approach and by observing the territory through which it passes.

We need to be aware of Bradley's blind spots and the facts and opinions that have been disproved or challenged in the years since he wrote. Once we adjust our focus to take account of these, his criticism becomes more remarkable and persuasive; with appropriate expectations, we can then build on his unquestionable discoveries. For example, we are unlikely to pursue the concept of a 'great man' as Bradley did, and yet we share readily his interest in the sources of intellectual power and personal domination, adding our later awareness of the horrors and terrors that a few charismatic, gifted and ambitious men can bring upon others. We may not be so concerned as he was to trace the workings of a God, fate, destiny, or some hypothetical 'supreme power' that shapes men's end, but the plays often speak about these matters and Bradley's argument about their importance will help us to enter into the minds of the persons of the plays while maintaining, as Bradley did, the beliefs or agnosticism that we bring to our studies.

Bradley's special interests and the blind spots need to be negotiated with care because they do not always draw attention to themselves. He was so interested in 'heroes' that he paid little attention to lesser persons and the part they played in a play's argument or the audience's experience of the entire play in performance. For example, when we hear of the cruelty and horrors perpetrated by Macbeth and see their effect on himself and others can we conclude as Bradley did that his 'greatness of soul' is the 'highest existence' that we know? Our response to *Hamlet* is bound to be affected by the arrival of Fortinbras, accompanied by his army and the English Ambassadors, and by the sound of cannon shot as four Captains lift up Hamlet's corpse. These visual and aural effects take considerable time to enact as they complete significant story lines and compete with spoken words for our attention. Surely a reader or critic with the 'eager mind' which Bradley requires should attempt to assess their contrasting effects, as well as dwelling on the exceptional qualities of Hamlet's speeches and the mysteries of his consciousness.

Bradley is most rewarding as a critic when we can see beyond the horizons and fixed ideas of his mind. Part II of this book presents his judgements on individual plays and demonstrates the exceptionally detailed and performative engagement with the texts in which their lasting value lies. Having regard to how he worked, we can follow where he leads, towards a view of the plays that is grounded in their presentation of persons who think and feel with a complexity similar to our own, but finer and more intense, and as they are engaged in crucial and awesome action beyond our experience. When we add a concern for the wider context of the narrative and its social and political implications, and when we add more visual, spatial and physical understanding of performance, his judgements can be the start of further exploration into the minds and sensations of the speakers, and modify our response to issues raised by a play's text and by the performances of an entire theatre company.

The concise presentation of Bradley's book that follows offers extensive passages of his most illuminating criticism and follows closely the course of his argument about each of the four major tragedies. But his argument with other opinions that are now discredited and his incomplete and sometimes – we now know – inaccurate accounts of Shakespeare's intellectual context are almost entirely excluded. Most of his more sentimental and biased accounts of the plays' characters are also dropped. The result is necessarily a patchwork but it should give the reader a ready entrance to what is most durable in Bradley's book without losing the frequent sensitivity and enthusiasm of his writing.

Shakespearean Tragedy deals only with the four tragedies that Bradley considered to be 'great' but this shortened version of his book concludes with passages taken from Bradley's lectures on *Coriolanus* and *Antony and Cleopatra*. Published a few years after his ground-breaking study and in anthologies that were not subsequently republished, these have not commanded such attention. But the two Roman tragedies extended the reach of his criticism in two significant ways. Both brought political issues to the forefront and, at crucial moments, silent elements of performance draw all attention. If his major work had considered six and not four tragedies, some of its conclusions might have been different.

PART I
Practical study and criticism

CHAPTER ONE

Verbal and Physical Imagery

Bradley's *Shakespearean Tragedy* is dedicated 'To my students' and carries the subtitle 'Lectures on Hamlet, Othello, King Lear [and] Macbeth'. A Preface further explains that the lectures are 'based on a selection from materials used in teaching at Liverpool, Glasgow, and Oxford'. The book's contents had been tested on a variety of listeners, repeatedly reconsidered, and cut down to what their author thought most necessary to communicate. And the process of reflection continued with the addition of long explanatory and often exploratory notes. Today most books about Shakespeare are written by teachers but at the beginning of the last century the long gestation and practical testing of this book were remarkable and signalled a new kind of attention to Shakespeare's plays, one that was both prolonged and personally engaged. Several times Bradley says that the plays should be read with an 'eager mind', and he implied that his book needed a similar mixture of diligence and excitement. More specifically Shakespeare's texts should be read as if they were one long continuous poem, written with the finesse and intensity of lyric poetry. Following the expectation of the romantic poets of the previous century, he expected Shakespeare to 'load every rift . . . with ore' (John Keats, letter to Shelley, August 1820). In the same spirit as Coleridge's *Biographia Literaria* (1817), he closely examined Shakespeare's imagery for the associations and reflections it brought to a reader's mind and the suggestion it gave of thoughts and feelings not directly or consciously expressed.

Since the 1930s many critics have taken the same approach. Caroline Spurgeon's *Shakespeare's Imagery and What It Tells Us* (1935) and H. W. Clemen's *The Development of Shakespeare's Imagery* (1936, translated from the German in 1951) marked out the way and soon a careful dissection of a play's verbal imagery was used to reveal meanings, implications, and intellectual issues not previously recognized. For example, Cleanth Brooks argued that Shakespeare's texts required the same subtle investigation and exegesis as the complex, 'metaphysical' poetry of John Donne: failing that, they could not be understood. Bradley had said much the same:

■ Where his power or art is fully exerted it really does resemble that of nature. It organizes and vitalizes its product from the centre outward to the minutest markings on the surface, so that when you turn upon it the most searching light you can command, when you dissect it and apply to it the test of a microscope, still you find in it nothing formless, general or vague, but everywhere structure, character, individuality. In this his great things, which seem to come whenever they are wanted, have no companions in literature except the few greatest things in Dante; and it is a fatal error to allow his carelessness elsewhere to make one doubt whether here one is not seeking more than can be found. It is very possible to look for subtlety in the wrong place in Shakespeare, but in the right places it is not possible to find too much.   (p. 54) □

Bradley's study of imagery is marked apart from that of many later critics by the connection he perceived between verbal imagery and physical on-stage action. He was also aware that the value of any particular moment depends on its position in the progress of the drama. Here is his account of Ophelia's speeches and on-stage performance:

■ To the persons in the play, as to the readers of it, she brings the thought of flowers. 'Rose of May' Laertes names her.

> Lay her in the earth,
> And from her fair and unpolluted flesh
> May violets spring!

– so he prays at her burial. 'Sweets to the sweet' the Queen murmurs, as she scatters flowers on the grave . . .   (p. 118) □

From his study of the verbal and physical imagery of a play Bradley was able to write about sensations, impressions, imaginary 'pictures', 'atmospheres', and all manner of thoughts that are not consciously formed or recognized by the persons of the drama. He was paying attention to those elements in a reader's or an audience's experience of the play that are real enough but have little to do with argument or narrative, that are intangible and yet unmistakable. Such perceptions may occur only fleetingly in an instant and yet Bradley shows that they accumulate and grow in power so that they come to influence almost every other aspect of an audience's response, and never more so than in *Macbeth*:

■ A Shakespearean tragedy, as a rule, has a special tone or atmosphere of its own, quite perceptible, however difficult to describe. The effect of this atmosphere is marked with unusual strength in *Macbeth*. It is due to a variety of influences which combine with those just noticed, so that, acting and reacting, they form a whole; and the desolation of the blasted heath, the design of the Witches, the guilt in the hero's soul, the darkness of the night, seem to emanate from one and the same source. This effect is strengthened by a multitude of small touches, which at the moment may be little noticed but still leave their mark on the imagination. We may approach the consideration of the characters and the action by distinguishing some of the ingredients of this general effect.

Darkness, we may even say blackness, broods over this tragedy. It is remarkable that almost all the scenes which at once recur to memory take place either at night or in some dark spot. The vision of the dagger, the murder of Duncan, the murder of Banquo, the sleep-walking of Lady Macbeth, all come in night-scenes. The Witches dance in the thick air of a storm, or, 'black and midnight hags', receive Macbeth in a cavern. The blackness of night is to the hero a thing of fear, even of horror; and that which he feels becomes the spirit of the play. The faint glimmerings of the western sky at twilight are here menacing: it is the hour when the traveller hastens to reach safety in his inn and when Banquo rides homeward to meet his assassins; the hour when 'light thickens', when 'night's black agents to their prey do rouse', when the wolf begins to howl, and the owl to scream, and withered murder steals forth to his work. Macbeth bids the stars hide their fires that his 'black' desires may be concealed; Lady Macbeth calls on thick night to come, palled in the dunnest smoke of hell. The moon is down and no stars shine when Banquo, dreading the dreams of the coming night, goes unwillingly to bed, and leaves Macbeth to wait for the summons of the little bell. When the next day should dawn, its light is 'strangled', and 'darkness does the face of earth entomb'. In the whole drama the sun seems to shine only twice; first, in the beautiful but ironical passage where Duncan sees the swallows flitting round the castle of death; and, afterwards, when at the close the avenging army gathers to rid the earth of its shame. Of the many slighter touches which deepen this effect I notice only one. The failure of nature in Lady Macbeth is marked by her fear of darkness; 'she has light by her continually'. And in the one phrase of fear that escapes her lips even in sleep, it is of the darkness of the place of torment that she speaks.   (pp. 253–4) □

Bradley has paid attention to 'a multitude of small touches' that, unless a reader seeks them out, will 'be little noticed but still leave their mark on the imagination'. Their effect on the actors' performance may be surreptitious but, inevitably, it colours how the words are spoken, and in turn influences physical performance. In certain scenes – after the murder, in the sleepwalking, or the solitary moments in the midst of the final battle – the movement from image to image, thought to thought, depends entirely on these unwilled and irrational movements of the mind. And Bradley remained alert to alternative sensations so that he continued:

■ The atmosphere of *Macbeth*, however, is not that of unrelieved blackness. On the contrary, as compared with *King Lear* and its cold dim gloom, *Macbeth* leaves a decided impression of colour; it is really the impression of a black night broken by flashes of light and colour, sometimes vivid and even glaring. They are the lights and colours of the thunderstorm in the first scene; of the dagger hanging before Macbeth's eyes and glittering alone in the midnight air; of the torch borne by the servant when he and his lord come upon Banquo cross-ing the castle-court to his room; of the torch, again, which Fleance carried to light his father to death, and which was dashed out by one of the murderers; of the torches that flared in the hall on the face of the Ghost and the blanched cheeks of Macbeth; of the flames beneath the boiling caldron from which the apparitions in the cavern rose; of the taper which showed to the Doctor and Gentlewoman the wasted face and blank eyes of Lady Macbeth. And, above all, the colour is the colour of blood. It cannot be an accident that the image of blood is forced upon us continually, not merely by the events them-selves, but by full descriptions, and even by reiteration of the word in unlikely parts of the dialogue. The Witches, after their first wild appearance, have hardly quitted the stage when there staggers onto it a 'bloody man', gashed with wounds. His tale is of a hero whose 'bran-dished steel smoked with bloody execution', 'carved out a passage' to his enemy, and 'unseam'd him from the nave to the chaps'. And then he tells of a second battle so bloody that the combatants seemed as if they 'meant to bathe in reeking wounds'. What metaphors! What a dreadful image is that with which Lady Macbeth greets us almost as she enters, when she prays the spirits of cruelty so to thicken her blood that pity cannot flow along her veins! What pictures are those of the murderer appearing at the door of the banquet-room with Banquo's 'blood upon his face'; of Banquo himself 'with twenty trenched gashes on his head', or 'blood-bolter'd' and smiling in derision at his murderer; of Macbeth, gazing at his hand, and watching it dye the whole green ocean red; of Lady Macbeth, gazing at hers, and stretch-ing it away from her face to escape the smell of blood that all the perfumes of Arabia will not subdue! The most horrible lines in the whole tragedy are those of her shuddering cry, 'Yet who would have thought the old man to have had so much blood in him?' And it is not only at such moments that these images occur. Even in the quiet conversation of Malcolm and Macduff, Macbeth is imagined as holding a bloody sceptre, and Scotland as a country bleeding and receiving every day a new gash added to her wounds. It is as if the poet saw the whole story through an ensanguined mist, and as if it stained the very blackness of the night. When Macbeth, before Banquo's murder, invokes night to scarf up the tender eye of pitiful day, and to tear in pieces the great bond that keeps him pale, even the invisible hand that is to tear the bond is imagined as covered with blood. ☐

This discussion of images, impressions, and 'atmosphere' is part of a more traditional criticism when linked to the progress of narrative and the sequence of on-stage action:

■ Let us observe another point. The vividness, magnitude, and violence of the imagery in some of these passages are characteristic of *Macbeth* almost throughout; and their influence contributes to form its atmosphere. Images like those of the babe torn smiling from the breast and dashed to death; of pouring the sweet milk of concord into hell; of the earth shaking in fever; of the frame of things disjointed; of sorrows striking heaven on the face, so that it resounds and yells out like syllables of dolour; of the mind lying in restless ecstasy on a rack; of the mind full of scorpions; of the tale told by an idiot, full of sound and fury; – all keep the imagination moving on a 'wild and violent sea', while it is scarcely for a moment permitted to dwell on thoughts of peace and beauty. In its language, as in its action, the drama is full of tumult and storm. Whenever the Witches are present we see and hear a thunder-storm: when they are absent we hear of shipwrecking storms and direful thunders; of tempests that blow down trees and churches, castles, palaces and pyramids; of the frightful hurricane of the night when Duncan was murdered; of the blast on which pity rides like a new-born babe, or on which Heaven's cherubim are horsed. There is thus something magnificently appropriate in the cry 'Blow, wind! Come wrack!' with which Macbeth, turning from the sight of the moving wood of Birnam, bursts from his castle. He was borne to his throne on a whirlwind, and the fate he goes to meet comes on the wings of storm. (pp. 253–6) ☐

CHAPTER TWO

Subtextual Meanings, Tensions and Sensations

Although Bradley knew nothing of the actor training of Constantin Stanislavski (1863–1938) or the psychology of Sigmund Freud (1856–1939), his interest in unspoken, unwilled, and unconscious elements of drama was in tune with the revaluation of words, unconscious motivations, and the presentation of self that was to be a mark of twentieth-century thought, social studies, and acting theory. But his interest in the subtextual life of a playtext also had contemporary parallels nearer home in the compellingly truthful performances of such star actors as Macready and Irving, Sarah Siddons and Ellen Terry. As these actors prepared their performances, they studied with great care those same details of a text that to others would seem 'inconsistent, indistinct, feeble, exaggerated'. Bradley was like them when he looked for possible evidence of 'some unusual trait in character, some abnormal movement of mind, only surprising to us because we understand so very much less of human nature than Shakespeare did' (p. 54).

This way of reading a text led him to make judgements that literary scholars have sometimes – and even recently – condemned as too subtle or irrelevant because not supported by the text in so many words. Throughout the mid-twentieth century he was faulted for treating the persons of a play as if they were actually breathing and alive in their minds but today it is that criticism of his method that seems ill-considered and perverse. Now that acting has become a subject for research and teaching in universities, texts that were written for performance are better understood. Bradley set out to study a playtext as actors do in rehearsal (see p. 27, below) and can help us to do the same. He sometimes exaggerated small details and gave too much weight to accidental or personal responses but the direction and ambition of his criticism have increasingly been judged irreproachable and, indeed, obligatory. He had entered difficult and uncertain territory when he sought to understand the plays as scripts for performance but this is ground that must be possessed if Shakespeare's plays are to be studied in the element for which they were written.

Bradley also knew that he had to judge according to his own experience and that he could be wrong. For example, he was ready to condemn the Player's speech about Pyrrhus in *Hamlet* as an example of crude bombast and therefore defective, but in the next sentence he confessed:

■ To me at any rate the metaphors in 'now is he total gules' and 'mincing with his sword her husband's limbs' are more disturbing than any of the bombast. (p. 323) □

He then quotes similarly grotesque images in widely admired speeches from *Othello, Macbeth, Troilus and Cressida* and *Romeo and Juliet* in which Shakespeare was not imitating a style different from his own (pp. 323–4).

Bradley's theatrical and experiential criticism encouraged his readers to *hear* the dialogue as it became speech in an imaginary performance and to judge its effect as an instinctive response of the speaker to the pressures of the dramatic moment. So, for example, he recognized ambiguities and sequences of underlying thought as Shakespeare's means of expressing reactions that remain unspoken. For instance, his comments on Hamlet's words and how he uses them, when he encounters Claudius apparently deep in prayer:

■ Now might I do it pat, now he is praying:
And now I'll do it: and so he goes to heaven:
And so am I revenged. That would be scanned.

. . . The first five words he utters, 'Now might I do it', show that he has no effective *desire* to 'do it'; and in the little sentences that follow, and the long pauses between them, the endeavour at a resolution, and the sickening return of melancholic paralysis, however difficult a task they set to the actor, are plain enough to a reader. (p. 98) □

But Bradley was no ordinary reader. In effect, the critic has attempted to enter the mind of the speaker in order to explain both words and syntax. In a note he adds. 'I am inclined to think that the note of interrogation put after "revenged" in a late Quarto is right.'

Bradley has also been criticized for trying to reconstruct events that pre-dated those presented in the play but, here again, he had read the text for its implications as well as its direct statements. The title of an essay of 1933 by L. C. Knights, 'How many children had Lady Macbeth?' was intended as a rebuke to Bradley's interest in a question that is not formulated in the play. But such enquiries derive from the text and their relevance for the actor (and subsequently for an audience) can hardly be doubted. How does Lady Macbeth – and Macbeth – speak of children: with what longing or with what fears? For Bradley, a more basic rephrasing of the question would be 'Why should she, at this instant, have thought of suckling an infant?'

Another example is Bradley's question concerning Hamlet's life immediately before the start of the play, which he considered in a long Note B (pp. 310–13). Did the prince remain as a student at Wittenberg until called back for his father's funeral or did the arrival of Horatio, Rosencrantz and Guildenstern awaken unexpected memories of a student life that he had relinquished as many as ten years before? These are not irrelevant questions because Hamlet's behaviour and his intellectual and political involvement in the action will be very different according to the answers that are given by the actor or reader. Should he be judged as a prince who had insisted on remaining a student until he was thirty years old, insulating himself from political and social responsibilities, or is he familiar with the company of kings and used to public gaze? In other words, is Ophelia reporting common opinion or is she fantasizing when she calls him the 'expectancy and rose of the fair state . . .' (III.i.152–4)? If he has lived at Elsinore along with his mother and father, he will think as a 'courtier' and understand the subtleties and politics of court life; he will also have become skilled in self-defence and learnt to think as a 'soldier', as well as a 'scholar'. If, however, he has remained a student for ten years at Wittenberg – Martin Luther's university and renowned for reformist opinions – he will have been caught up in the bettering of his mind and lived where self-doubt and religious argument were current and urgent matters of concern. These two opposed readings of the text are of undeniable critical importance.

Here textual questions are also raised by Bradley's interest in character and the unspoken life of the drama. The first Quarto, of 1600, implies that Hamlet is about nineteen years old but the second Quarto, of 1604–5, and the first Folio, of 1623, both give his age as exactly thirty (see V.i.138–58). Does the early text represent Shakespeare's first idea of the sort of person Hamlet is, and was that modified later, as in the later texts? If this is how the play was written over a number of years, do the later texts retain some other readings that have survived, uncorrected, from the early version in which 'young Hamlet' (I.i.170) was *very* young? Does a thirty-year-old Hamlet love an Ophelia who is 'in the morn and liquid dew of youth' (I.iii.41) or did Shakespeare decide that he was older *after* he had written her part in the play?

What is not said or might have been said differently can only be inferred from the text and therefore, to some degree, Bradley's arguments are speculative and subject to his own predilections and choices. But they also give rise to questions that are a necessary part of an actor's study and the answers the actor gives will influence an audience's experience of the play in performance. These are reasons enough for any reader's attention. To stay with Hamlet for an example, in the Graveyard of Act V, scene i:

■ he stands in a most perilous position. On one side of him is the King, whose safety depends on his death, and who has done his best to murder him; on the other, Laertes, whose father and sister he has sent to their graves, and of whose behaviour and probable attitude he must surely be informed by Horatio. What is required of him, therefore, if he is not to perish with his duty undone, is the utmost wariness and the swiftest resolution. Yet it is not too much to say that, except when Horatio forces the matter on his attention, he shows no consciousness of this position. He muses in the graveyard on the nothingness of life and fame, and the base uses to which our dust returns, whether it be a court jester's or a world-conqueror's. He learns that the open grave over which he muses has been dug for the woman he loved; and he suffers one terrible pang, from which he gains relief in frenzied words and frenzied action – action which must needs intensify, if that were possible, the fury of the man whom he has, however unwittingly, so cruelly injured. Yet he appears utterly unconscious that he has injured Laertes at all, and asks him:

What is the reason that you use me thus?

And as the sharpness of the first pang passes, the old weary misery returns, and he might almost say to Ophelia, as he does to her brother:

I loved you ever: but it is no matter.

'It is no matter': *nothing* matters.   (pp. 106–7)   □

When reading Shakespeare's plays, Bradley wanted 'to realize fully and exactly the inner movements [of the mind] which produced these words and no other, these deeds and no other, at each particular moment' (p. xlvii). By this means, study of a play's text leads on to a consideration of its characters and their beliefs, hopes and fears, together with the freedom and controlling pressures of their lives. In other words, studying the details of a text as Bradley did will lead on to a close study of the persons of the drama as they belong to a particular group of persons, and of the forces at work in their history and individual lives.

The long Note L, about Othello's jealousy, exemplifies the complex nature of Bradley's verbal study. The time when any words are used is taken into account, as well as their changing meanings, the intentions behind them, the persons to whom they are addressed. He knew that meaning and effect depended on their social and political context and, although he did not pursue this line of enquiry very far, he offers questions to present-day critics who have much deeper and wider access to Elizabethan and Jacobean culture. In this note Bradley also refers to the performances of gifted actors and to Shakespeare's use of a difficult phrase in a similar situation in a quite different text:

■ One reason why some readers think Othello 'easily jealous' is that they completely misinterpret him in the early part of this scene. They fancy that he is alarmed and suspicious the moment he hears Iago mutter 'Ha! I like not that', as he sees Cassio leaving Desdemona (III.iii.35). But, in fact, it takes a long time for Iago to excite surprise, curiosity, and then grave concern – by no means yet jealousy – even about Cassio; and it is still longer before Othello understands that Iago is suggesting doubts about Desdemona too. ('Wronged' in 143 certainly does not refer to her, as 154 and 162 show.) Nor, even at 171, is the exclamation 'O misery' meant for an expression of Othello's own present feelings; as his next speech clearly shows, it expresses an *imagined* feeling, as also the speech which elicits it professes to do (for Iago would not have dared here to apply the term 'cuckold' to Othello). In fact it is not until Iago hints that Othello, as a foreigner, might easily be deceived, that he is seriously disturbed about Desdemona.

Salvini played this passage, as might be expected, with entire understanding. Nor have I ever seen it seriously misinterpreted on the stage. I gather from the Furness Variorum that Fechter and Edwin Booth took the same view as Salvini. Actors have to ask themselves what was the precise state of mind expressed by the words they have to repeat. But many readers never think of asking such a question.

The lines which probably do most to lead hasty or unimaginative readers astray are those at 90, where, on Desdemona's departure, Othello exclaims to himself:

> Excellent wretch! Perdition catch my soul
> But I do love thee! and when I love thee not,
> Chaos is come again.

He is supposed to mean by the last words that his love is *now* suspended by suspicion, whereas, in fact, in his bliss, he has so totally forgotten Iago's 'Ha! I like not that', that the tempter has to begin all over again. The meaning is, 'If ever I love thee not, Chaos will have come again'. The feeling of insecurity is due to the excess of *joy*, as in the wonderful words after he rejoins Desdemona at Cyprus (II.i.191):

> If it were now to die,
> 'Twere now to be most happy: for, I fear
> My soul hath her content so absolute
> That not another comfort like to this
> Succeeds in unknown fate.

If any reader boggles at the use of the present in 'Chaos is come again', let him observe 'succeeds' in the lines just quoted, or let him look at the parallel passage in *Venus and Adonis*, 1019:

> For, he being dead, with him is beauty slain:
> And, beauty dead, black Chaos comes again.

Venus does not know that Adonis is dead when she speaks thus. (pp. 340–1) ☐

CHAPTER THREE

Action, Narrative and Plot

Guided by his knowledge of Greek drama and Aristotle's *Poetics*, Bradley understood tragedy to be the 'imitation of an action' culminating in resolution and judgement. How Shakespeare had handled the principal events of a play's story and brought all to a comprehensive conclusion would therefore provide the backbone of his criticism. He would ask 'what actually happens in the play' (p. 85) in order to sharpen his reading of a text and his understanding of character. For example, to counter the current view that Hamlet was 'one-sidedly reflective and indisposed to action' – an interpretation propounded by Coleridge and the German scholar and translator August Wilhelm Schlegel (1767–1845) – Bradley cited on-stage action as evidence:

■ He must always have been fearless – in the play he appears insensible to fear of any ordinary kind. And, finally, he must have been quick and impetuous in action; for it is downright impossible that the man we see rushing after the Ghost, killing Polonius, dealing with the King's commission on the ship, boarding the pirate, leaping into the grave, executing his final vengeance, could *ever* have been shrinking or slow in an emergency. Imagine Coleridge doing any of these things! (p. 79) □

Schooled by Greek example and recognizing Shakespeare's debt to Seneca and classical dramatic forms, Bradley's study of dialogue and of action, narrative and plot showed how a play's structure gave to its audience or reader a deep and subtle understanding of its major character or characters, a perception that becomes deeper and more secure during the course of performance and culminates in a final judgement that identifies what Aristotle had called the hero's 'tragic flaw'. His reading of Greek and Latin tragedies, backed up by Aristotle's theorizing, encouraged him to pay little attention to those elements of a tragedy in which its hero was not engaged or that were not immediately relevant to his actions. With the same bias, he analysed the action and plotting of a play in terms of a conflict between good and evil as represented in its main character or characters:

■ Shakespeare's general plan . . . is to show one set of forces advancing, in secret or open opposition to the other, to some decisive success, and then driven downward to defeat by the reaction it provokes. And the advantages of this plan, as seen in such a typical instance as *Julius Caesar*, are manifest. It conveys the movement of the conflict to the mind with great clearness and force. It helps to produce the impression that in his decline and fall the doer's act is returning on his own head. And, finally, as used by Shakespeare, it makes the first half of the play intensely interesting and dramatic. Action which effects a striking change in an existing situation is naturally watched with keen interest; and this we find in some of these tragedies. And the spectacle, which others exhibit, of a purpose forming itself and, in spite of outward obstacles and often of inward resistance, forcing its way onward to a happy consummation or a terrible deed, not only gives scope to that psychological subtlety in which Shakespeare is scarcely rivalled, but is also dramatic in the highest degree.   (pp. 38–9) □

But even as he proposed this view of dramatic structure, Bradley acknowledged that Shakespeare did not always use it well: 'when the crisis has been reached there come difficulties and dangers'. The 'decisive success' that comes mid-way in the action of a Shakespearean tragedy calls for a pause and slacking of interest before the final catastrophe:

■ How can deliberations between Octavius, Antony and Lepidus, between Malcolm and Macduff, between the Capulets, between Laertes and the King, keep us at the pitch, I do not say of the crisis, but even of the action which led up to it? Good critics . . . have held that some of [Shakespeare's] greatest tragedies fall off in the Fourth Act, and that one or two never wholly recover themselves. And I believe most readers would find, if they examined their impressions, that to their minds *Julius Caesar*, *Hamlet*, *King Lear* and *Macbeth* have all a tendency to 'drag' in this section of the play, and that the first and perhaps also the last of these four fail even in the catastrophe to reach the height of the greatest scenes that have preceded the Fourth Act. (pp. 39–40) □

If the tragedies are judged by Bradley's standards these are indeed faults of construction, which he tried to justify in terms of counteraction or 'counter stroke', or the introduction of new and sometimes false expectation, emotional variety, pathetic contrast, or humorous relief. But even if a reader or audience shares Bradley's keen interest in danger and crisis, a contrast that lessens the tension or some uncertainty about the direction in which the author is leading can strengthen the most obvious satisfactions that a play gives. In continuous action, as Shakespeare has Portia say in *The Merchant of Venice*, 'Nothing is good, I see, without respect' (V.i.99): the 'true' value of any one incident in an audience's experience may depend on other elements than dramatic pitch and excitement.

Believing conflict to be the basis of a tragedy, Bradley emphasized crisis and climax, even when the narrative and structure of the play do not lend themselves to a final concentrated effect but offer a wider view with the introduction of new persons or further considerations. He saw *Macbeth* as imitating the intensity and sensationalism of Seneca by giving almost all attention to the two principal characters. The contrasting faith and courage of the Siwards, father and son, are not mentioned in his account of the tragedy's last scenes; the response of the two Murderers to Macbeth's interrogation (III.i.73–139) is passed over without comment; Ross's growing sense of responsibility throughout all five Acts is not noticed, nor is Seyton's unusually independent presence alongside Macbeth immediately before his last fight and death. Malcolm's detailed account of the moral and social consequences of unbridled power and the test he makes of Macduff's loyalty scarcely figure in Bradley's account of the play although together they account for 71 lines of carefully wrought verse that account for almost a third of the scene immediately preceding the final Act.

Earlier critics had already commented on the Porter of Act II, scene iii, and so Bradley paid exceptional attention to this brief role. Because the episode did not 'make me smile', he argued that it was not meant to do so: Shakespeare must have written it less humorously than he might so that no one except groundlings would 'forget for a moment what has preceded and what must follow' (p. 303). This was not the only place, in Bradley's view, 'that Shakespeare was hurried, and, throwing all his weight on the principal characters, did not exert himself in dealing with the rest' (p. 297).

In the two Lectures on *Othello*, the story of Roderigo is not mentioned although we may see analogies with the main events as well as contrasts to them: this man, who is foolish in many ways, will risk everything for love of Desdemona and, as a result, loses his life. Of the Clown who enters at the start of Act III and again immediately after Othello has fallen into Iago's trap, Bradley remarks, 'we hardly attend to him and quickly forget him' (p. 132) as if he saw no purpose in his presence. Bradley's attention is given freely to persons other than the hero only when they are directly caught up with him or her in striking dramatic, emotional and moral conflict. So Emilia is crucial to his view of the tragedy:

■ She says what we long to say. . . . And who has not felt in the last scene how her glorious carelessness of her own life, and her outbursts against Othello – even that most characteristic one,

She was too fond of her most filthy bargain –

lift the overwhelming weight of calamity that oppresses us, and bring us an extraordinary lightening of the heart?   (p. 180) □

But Emilia's pragmatic and even-handed view of marriage – 'Let husbands know / Their wives have sense like them' (IV.iii.91ff.) – plays no part in Bradley's view of the play, nor does Desdemona's silent attention to what she is saying at this time of exceptional intimacy. Bradley, like his Greek masters, cared most about conflict, moral judgement and 'greatness of spirit', and little about a wider and progressively revealing view of society and politics that reflects the life-experiences of the play's audience. At the start of an introductory chapter on 'The Substance of Shakespearean Tragedy', he noted that:

■ such a tragedy brings before us a considerable number of persons (many more than the persons in a Greek play, unless the members of the Chorus are reckoned among them); but it is pre-eminently the story of one person, the 'hero', or at most of two, the 'hero' and 'heroine'.   (p. 2) □

The episodes and characters that Bradley did not analyse with his customary care are a measure of what is missing from his account of action, narrative, and plot and an indication of Shakespeare's adherence to a less classical and hero-centric view of dramatic narrative. He failed to see how strongly Shakespeare's tragedies belonged to a native and medieval tradition of narrative drama. Rather than being an imitation of any one action, these plays tell a story with many threads. Minor characters and changes of location are used to create a sequence of separate episodes that either challenge the resources of the principal character or characters or provide illuminating contrasts. Rather than presenting conflict and crisis, the action can be seen as a journey or quest undertaken by the tragic hero that gives rise to a series of analogies and incidents that extend an audience's understanding of the issues involved and of the society in which the action takes place. In this tradition, Shakespeare's 'faults' and 'counter strokes' can be seen as the means by which he steadily widened the dramatic focus to include the consequences of the hero's actions for the society through which the narrative moves and to present thoughts and feelings that belong to the day-to-day lives of persons who are less exceptional and even mundane in comparison with the activator of the dramatic action. In its adherence to this native and narrative form, Shakespearean tragedy offers a view of an entire world, the hero being the most continuous point of focus in that view as he or she draws the action and attention forward. By following this double pattern, Shakespearean tragedy widens as well as deepens the experience of audience or reader.

The medieval tradition was very much alive in Elizabethan and Jacobean drama, in comedies and histories, as well as tragedies. Marlowe's *Tamburlane* and numerous other Elizabethan plays that are based on romantic or historical narratives are evidence of its lasting influence but Bradley failed to recognize this even though the double plot of *King Lear* obviously contravenes his classical idea of what a tragedy should be. Not only does its last Act contain much that does not intensify dramatic focus on the hero, but the hero has been given little to say as other characters and other business occupy the stage. Bradley wrote dismissively of 'the overloading which distresses us in *King Lear*' and faulted it as 'imperfectly dramatic' (pp. 298 and 185). He was, nevertheless, convinced of the play's 'imaginative' truth and moments of great intensity. He also realized that the presence of Gloucester and his sons provided 'contrast' and 'comparison' with the story of Lear and his daughters. The result was:

■ that feeling which haunts us in *King Lear*, as though we were witnessing something universal – a conflict not so much of particular persons as of the powers of good and evil in the world. And the treatment of many of the characters confirms this feeling. Considered simply as psychological studies few of them, surely, are of the highest interest. (p. 196) □

While recognizing the width of dramatic focus in this tragedy, Bradley still saw its action as a conflict although not within one leading character: here two groups of persons are involved in a conflict of good and evil:

■ the radical differences of the two species are emphasized in broad hard strokes; and the two are set in conflict, almost as if Shakespeare, like Empedocles, were regarding Love and Hate as the two ultimate forces of the universe. (p. 197) □

It is instructive to see with what difficulty Bradley makes Shakespeare conform to classical notions of dramatic form, especially if his view is offset and complemented by giving attention to those features which he forgets or does not heed. With his attention focused on their heroes, he did not see that these plays present a model of what was then the present-day world and everyday lives, as well as a conflict in the life of a few exceptional men and women. This wide-focused and narrative form of drama was dominant in England in earlier times when God's ways with men and women were displayed in great detail and at length in the hugely popular miracle plays.

But multiple action, varied characters and the pressures and pleasures of actual contemporary lives were not old-fashioned or casual survivals in Shakespeare's tragedies. They were elements to which he gave new and distinctive life in a new context and they would be copied abundantly in the tragedies of his younger successors, John Webster, Thomas Middleton, and John Ford chief among them.

The re-creation of lived experience and the excitation of topical responses in a wide-focused narrative drama give a theatrical pleasure that can draw audiences in ways that do not depend upon a hero-centred pattern of conflict and crisis. It is a form of drama with strong traditions throughout the world and reaching back many centuries. According to a two-thousand-year-old theatre manual, the *Natyasastra*, the gods invented theatre in order to give pleasure and provide a view of the audience's own lives, as well as presenting superior persons and the gods themselves. At the end of the twentieth century a popular theatre, presenting persons of power alongside those who seem powerless, has been more soberly represented in the 'epic' theatre of Bertolt Brecht and other dramatists. When reading Bradley on the tragedies and following his exploration of a central action and dominant persons, it is instructive to seek out those elements and reactions that this critic has forgotten but which are often present, especially as the action comes to its end. In Shakespeare's day, everyday events and comparatively ordinary characters were among those elements in the plays that served a 'lively' art and encouraged acting that was 'to the life'. They are also likely to have given pleasure to the 'groundlings', the liveliest and least manageable members of an audience.

CHAPTER FOUR

Characters

Repeatedly, Bradley brought discussion of a play's characters to the test of his own experience and moral judgement, at the same time challenging his reader to do the same. He presented the persons of the drama as if they were his contemporaries on whose behalf he could argue. For example, 'Why should [Ophelia] not tell her father the whole story [of Hamlet's protestation of love] and give him an old letter which may help to convince the King and Queen?' (p. 120). He ridiculed less practical and less fair-minded opinion:

■ 'But she practised deception [we are told]; she even told a lie. Hamlet asked her where her father was, and she said he was at home, when he was really listening behind a curtain.' Poor Ophelia! It is considered angelic in Desdemona to say untruly that she killed herself, but most immoral or pusillanimous in Ophelia to tell *her* lie. I will not discuss these casuistical problems; but, if ever an angry lunatic asks me a question which I cannot answer truly without great danger to him and to one of my relations, I hope that grace may be given me to imitate Ophelia. □

What 'actually happens' in the play is again the touchstone for judgement:

■ Still, we are told, it was ridiculously weak in her to lose her reason. And here again her critics seem hardly to realize the situation, hardly to put themselves in the place of a girl whose lover, estranged from her, goes mad and kills her father. They seem to forget also that Ophelia must have believed that these frightful calamities were not mere calamities, but followed from *her* action in repelling her lover. Nor do they realize the utter loneliness that must have fallen on her. Of the three persons who were all the world to her, her father has been killed, Hamlet has been sent out of the country insane, and her brother is abroad. Horatio, when her mind gives way, tries to befriend her, but there is no sign of any previous relation between them, or of Hamlet's having commended her to his friend's care. What support she can gain from the Queen we can guess from the Queen's character, and from the fact that, when Ophelia is most helpless, the Queen shrinks from the very sight of her (IV.v.1). She was left, thus, absolutely alone, and if she looked for her brother's return (as she did, IV.v.70), she might reflect that it would mean danger to Hamlet.   (pp. 120–1) □

Close analysis of the text is always the basis of Bradley's study of character as it is of speech, narrative and action. And, similarly, he compares one moment with others, characters in one play with those in others; he is concerned with what is *not* said as well as with speech, and, when a play has more than one original edition, he considers all available versions. His discussion of Cordelia in the opening scene of *King Lear* exemplifies his customary care:

■ At a moment where terrible issues join, Fate makes on her the one demand which she is unable to meet. As I have already remarked in speaking of Desdemona, it was a demand which other heroines of Shakespeare could have met. Without loss of self-respect, and refusing even to appear to compete for a reward, they could have made the unreasonable old King feel that he was fondly loved. Cordelia cannot, because she is Cordelia. And so she is not merely rejected and banished, but her father is left to the mercies of her sisters. And the cause of her failure – a failure a thousand-fold redeemed – is a compound in which imperfection appears so intimately mingled with the noblest qualities that – if we are true to Shakespeare – we do not think either of justifying her or of blaming her: we feel simply the tragic emotions of fear and pity.

In this failure a large part is played by that obvious characteristic to which I have already referred. Cordelia is not, indeed, always tongue-tied, as several passages in the drama, and even in this scene, clearly show. But tender emotion, and especially a tender love for the person to whom she has to speak, makes her dumb. Her love, as she says, is more ponderous than her tongue:

> Unhappy that I am, I cannot heave
> My heart into my mouth.

This expressive word 'heave' is repeated in the passage which describes her reception of Kent's letter:

> Faith, once or twice she heaved the name of 'Father'
> Pantingly forth, as if it press'd her heart:

two or three broken ejaculations escape her lips, and she 'starts' away 'to deal with grief alone'. The same trait reappears with an ineffable beauty in the stifled repetitions with which she attempts to answer her father in the moment of his restoration:

Lear.   Do not laugh at me;
          For, as I am a man, I think this lady
          To be my child Cordelia.
Cor.   And so I am, I am.
Lear. Be your tears wet? yes, faith. I pray, weep not;
          If you have poison for me, I will drink it.
          I know you do not love me; for your sisters
          Have, as I so remember, done me wrong:
          You have some cause, they have not.
Cor.   No cause, no cause.

We see this trait for the last time, marked by Shakespeare with a decision clearly intentional, in her inability to answer one syllable to the last words we hear her father speak to her:

          No, no, no, no! Come, let's away to prison:
          We two alone will sing like birds i' the cage:
          When thou dost ask me blessing, I'll kneel down,
          And ask of thee forgiveness: so we'll live,
          And pray, and sing, and tell old tales, and laugh
          At gilded butterflies. . . .

She stands and weeps, and goes out with him silent. And we see her alive no more.   (pp. 241–3) □

The effusive expressions of sentiment in this passage show an emotional simplification found in other passages concerned with Shakespeare's heroines. Like his acceptance of royal prerogative, male superiority, class distinction, and the necessity of fighting wars, his confident references to the human soul, spiritual beauty, and 'ineffable goodness' carry an unquestioned sentiment that is unfamiliar to us and often sounds trite and empty. Inevitably we question his judgement but these attitudes were common among writers of his time and, being freely and, it seems, easily expressed, they are evidence of the personal basis of all Bradley's criticism, a sign that he wrote as he instinctively felt and that his judgements are based on his own personal sentiment. If we find that we cannot share in any or all of these feelings, his criticism will alert us to the need of making our own judgements – as he did – as we follow his insistent and questioning progress through the plays.

In treating the persons of the drama in this personal way, as if they were alive at the present time, Bradley's critical stance is very different from the historically informed and linguistically curious methods of much current criticism. But it is very similar to how actors prepare to perform a role by bringing their own life experience and questioning mind to the task of understanding the text. The plays were written for this individual exploration and personal identification. Actors may be more or less idiosyncratic, practical, or skilled, but in some measure all actors in all ages participate in the same kind of enquiry as Bradley customarily undertook.

While drawing on his own life-experiences, Bradley also recognized that the leading persons of the plays were involved in events more dangerous and more emotionally demanding than his own, beyond those of ordinary lives and the reach of ordinary conceptions:

■ His tragic characters are made of the stuff we find within ourselves and within the persons who surround them. But, by an intensification of the life which they share with others, they are raised above them; and the greatest are raised so far that, if we fully realize all that is implied in their words and actions, we become conscious that in real life we have known scarcely any one resembling them. Some, like Hamlet and Cleopatra, have genius. Others, like Othello, Lear, Macbeth, Coriolanus, are built on the grand scale; and desire, passion, or will attains in them a terrible force. In almost all we observe a marked one-sidedness, a predisposition in some particular direction; a total incapacity, in certain circumstances, of resisting the force which draws in this direction; a fatal tendency to identify the whole being with one interest, object, passion, or habit of mind.   (p. 12) □

This passage also illustrates Bradley's search for one predominant feeling, passion, or habit of mind in the persons Shakespeare created in the plays. He used all these terms and more to describe a permanent state of being that seeks satisfaction and expression in the course of the narrative, so that performance leads towards a final and revelatory manifestation of self. This recognition affects his view of the very structure of the plays and their cumulative effect on an audience. So essential is it to his criticism, that we should stop to ask whether this was, indeed, how Shakespeare conceived and developed individual character and how the plays work on an audience. Bradley had little doubt that it was, and we might add that, although Bradley had rejected the Christian view of life in which he had been brought up, the idea of a character's action leading towards a final moment of truth has similarities with ideas of a struggle between good and evil, an inevitable day of judgement, and a search for personal salvation that, in Shakespeare's England, were the basis of the daily rituals of the church, and the burden of its homilies and many sermons preached throughout the land.

CHAPTER FIVE

The Hero

From Bradley's interest in 'character' and the 'greatness' he saw in the tragic heroes, two conclusions followed. First, that Shakespeare was intent on demonstrating the nature of human 'greatness' so that, by the end of a tragedy, audiences and readers should 'realize the full power and reach of the soul' and his tragic heroes would awaken 'not only sympathy and pity, but admiration, terror, and awe' (p. 12). In this Bradley echoes Aristotle's formulation of tragedy as the imitation of an action involving the greatest of human beings, and considers Shakespeare's heroes as exceptions among lesser persons. Secondly, following what was then the usual translation of Aristotle's *hamartia*, he argued that a 'tragic flaw' brought about the death of the plays' heroes; in their lives, 'something is required which a smaller man might have given, but which the hero cannot give . . . and his error, joining with other causes, brings on him ruin' (p. 13). For Bradley this 'fatal imperfection or error' had crucial importance:

■ The tragic hero with Shakespeare, then, need not be 'good', though generally he is 'good' and therefore at once wins sympathy in his error. But it is necessary that he should have so much of greatness that in his error and fall we may be vividly conscious of the possibilities of human nature. Hence, in the first place, a Shakespearean tragedy is never, like some miscalled tragedies, depressing. No one ever closes the book with the feeling that man is a poor mean creature. He may be wretched and he may be awful, but he is not small.   (p. 14) □

This formulation of the moral and hero-centred nature of Shakespearean tragedy challenges a reader's response to both the texts and their theatrical effect. Are we able to identify an 'action' as the subject of each one of the tragedies and does this account for the experience the tragedies provide? Is our attention concentrated to this extent on the heroes and on their 'greatness'? At the end of a tragedy is an audience encouraged to identify a 'flaw' in the tragic hero? Pursuing those questions may not bring a reader to share Bradley's opinions but they will clarify and sharpen our response to the plays and challenge our judgement.

Bradley himself raises many of our questions because he was torn between his admiration for the 'spirit' or 'soul' – or we might say, the romance – of his heroes and his critical duty to find their basic fault. For example, after a description of Othello's cruel and deliberate murder of Desdemona, a reader might hesitate to accept Bradley's hyperboles in writing of his greatness of spirit but the difficulty of this judgement is not hidden: he knows that his view depends on the significant but speechless act of kissing a dead body, which, in performance, both actor and audience are left to interpret:

■ As he speaks those final words in which all the glory and agony of his life – long ago in India and Arabia and Aleppo, and afterwards in Venice, and now in Cyprus – seem to pass before us, like the pictures that flash before the eyes of a drowning man, a triumphant scorn for the fetters of the flesh and the littleness of all the lives that must survive him sweeps our grief away, and when he dies upon a kiss the most painful of all tragedies leaves us for the moment free from pain, and exulting in the power of 'love and man's unconquerable mind'. (pp. 147–8) □

Whereas Bradley located the main action of the tragedies within the minds and actions of the protagonists he noted that the contribution of accident or chance was greater towards the end of each play so that, as the narrative draws to a close, an inevitable fate seems to drive events forward: the prince, king, queen, wife, mistress, lover, brother, or warrior has no option but to face death and die. He emphasized 'a sense in Hamlet that he is in the hands of Providence' (p. 105) and saw the Witches in *Macbeth* as 'the witness of forces which never cease to work in the world around [Macbeth], and, on the instant of his surrender to them, entangle him inextricably in the web of Fate' (p. 292). By his study of Shakespeare's heroes Bradley had demonstrated how the enacted narratives of the plays raise the perennial questions of personal freedom and responsibility even more clearly than any words that are spoken.

CHAPTER SIX

Contexts

A work of art is not an island, entire of its self, but takes life and gains meanings from all its maker's works and from the far wider cultural context in which and for which it was made. Although *Shakespearean Tragedy* is structured around four plays, everything that Shakespeare wrote comes into the reckoning. As we have seen, Desdemona and Cordelia are produced as evidence against a current view of Ophelia, and, throughout Bradley's book, ancient Greek tragedies, poetry in several languages, current and earlier criticism, philosophy, psychology, and religion make occasional entries in his argument.

Bradley started his account of *Othello* by considering its action in relation to the intellectual and cultural context suggested by Shakespeare's other tragedies and by Milton's *Paradise Lost* and the *Oedipus Rex* of Sophocles:

■ *King Lear* is undoubtedly the tragedy which comes nearest to *Othello* in the impression of darkness and fatefulness, and in the absence of direct indications of any guiding power. But in *King Lear* . . . the conflict assumes proportions so vast that the imagination seems, as in *Paradise Lost*, to traverse spaces wider than the earth. In reading *Othello* the mind is not thus distended. It is more bound down to the spectacle of noble beings caught in toils from which there is no escape. . . . All this and much more seems to us quite natural, so potent is the art of the dramatist; but it confounds us with a feeling, such as we experience in the *Oedipus Tyrannus*, that for these star-crossed mortals . . . there is no escape from fate, and even with a feeling, absent from that play, that fate has taken sides with villainy. It is not surprising, therefore, that *Othello* should affect us as *Hamlet* and *Macbeth* never do, and as *King Lear* does only in slighter measure.   (pp. 134–5) □

While Shakespeare's other plays, as well as classical tragedy, and poetry in English and Italian make repeated appearances in Bradley's criticism there are, as we have seen, few references to English dramatists contemporary with Shakespeare. Students of today are less likely to underrate their influence but will find that Bradley, remarkably among critics of his own time, shared a more recent interest in audiences and a concern for a play's reception in performance. 'How would this text affect an audience?' was a question kept constantly in mind and, in consequence, he tried to account for certain puzzling moments in a play by reference to its cultural context – to what he understood of the beliefs and social practices of its first Elizabethan and Jacobean audiences. He was still more concerned with the effect of performance on audiences of his own time.

Both these audiences are invoked when considering whether the Ghost's reappearance in Gertrude's closet in Act III, scene iv, is a hallucination and not the same spirit come from the dead that is encountered in the first Act. Bradley dismissed the latter notion as:

■ **partly [due] to two mistakes, the substitution of our present intellectual atmosphere for the Elizabethan, and the notion that, because the Queen does not see and hear the Ghost, it is meant to be unreal. But a ghost, in Shakespeare's day, was able for any sufficient reason to confine its manifestation to a single person in a company; and here the sufficient reason, that of sparing the Queen, is obvious. (p. 102)** □

Bradley quotes only one later authority for this assertion without considering other renaissance ideas about hallucinations. Scholarship in his day had not searched far into the life and thought of Shakespeare's time and so a warning against too easy acceptance should be attached to all such contextual references in Bradley's *Shakespearean Tragedy*. Its usefulness in this respect is to draw attention to underlying intellectual issues and intruding assumptions of the present time.

Examples of Bradley's exposed position as a scholar of the period are found with regard to such issues as race, gender, marriage, religion, superstition, self-knowledge, and sexuality and sexual *mores*. Here his continuing value for a student lies in the exploration of the consequences of action that was basic to his critical method. Discussing Hamlet's 'duty' of revenge and the authority of his father's Ghost, Bradley cannot refer to any of the numerous books on the subject that have extended our knowledge of the wide range of beliefs that were current when the tragedy was written. His views need to be supplemented and corrected by Fredson Bowers' *Elizabethan Revenge Tragedy* (Princeton, 1940), Eleanor Prosser's *Hamlet and Revenge* (Stanford, 1967), Peter Mercer's '*Hamlet' and the Acting of Revenge* (London, 1987) and Stephen Greenblatt's *Hamlet in Purgatory* (Princeton, 2001). Bradley was content to assume that, in the context of the play and his time, Hamlet had a moral duty to kill Claudius:

■ Surely it is clear that, whatever we in the twentieth century may think about Hamlet's duty, we are meant in the play to assume that he *ought* to have obeyed the Ghost.   (p. 72) □

The Christian prohibition of revenge has no weight in his argument when set against the impression made by the progress of the play on reader or audience, but here and elsewhere his concern for the reception of a performance remains a useful caution against views that depend exclusively on a study of the words spoken or an isolated moment in a narrative.

When considering the Witches in *Macbeth*, Bradley refers to contemporary writings about their nature and power and is very aware of alternative beliefs. Text and action both come into his argument as he opens up various paths to an understanding of their role in the play:

■ On the one hand the Witches, whose contribution to the 'atmosphere' of *Macbeth* can hardly be exaggerated, are credited with far too great an influence upon the action; sometimes they are described as goddesses, or even as fates, whom Macbeth is powerless to resist. And this is perversion. On the other hand, we are told that, great as is their influence on the action, it is so because they are merely symbolic representations of the unconscious or half-conscious guilt in Macbeth himself. And this is inadequate.   (pp. 259) □

For Bradley the context extended from Reginald Scot's *Discovery of Witchcraft* (1584) and Holinshed's *Chronicles*, to Shakespeare's *Merry Wives*, *Hamlet* and *Othello*, Thomas Middleton's *The Witch*, the *Illiad* and, more generally and vaguely, the possible responses of a Jacobean audience. He concludes the debate by that appeal to experience which was a bracing and recurrent element in his criticism:

■ we need not fear, and indeed shall scarcely be able, to exaggerate the effect of the Witch-scenes in heightening and deepening the sense of fear, horror, and mystery which pervades the atmosphere of the tragedy.   (p. 265) □

The contribution that comedy makes to a tragedy is usually disregarded or dismissed on the grounds of its Elizabethan context, an exception being made for the Fool in *Lear*.

■ The theatrical fool or clown (we need not distinguish them here) was a sore trial to the cultured poet and spectator in Shakespeare's day. He came down from the Morality plays, and was beloved of the groundlings. His antics, his songs, his dances, his jests, too often unclean, delighted them, and did something to make the drama, what the vulgar, poor or rich, like it to be, a variety entertainment. Even if he confined himself to what was set down for him he often disturbed the dramatic unity of the piece; and the temptation to 'gag' was too strong for him to resist. . . . Shakespeare used him – we know to what effect – as he used all the other popular elements of the drama; but he abstained from introducing him into the Roman plays, and there is no fool in the last of the pure tragedies, *Macbeth*.   (pp. 235–6) □

Without the advantage of later research into the shifting meanings of *clown* and *fool* or the festive and carnival aspects of theatre, jokes and physical fooling are passed over so easily that a reader with a knowledge of the play is likely to become acutely conscious of the restrictions that Bradley accepted in his sober quest for the lasting significance of Shakespeare's tragedies.

Political issues of power and personal freedom are given almost no attention; neither are the realities of war or the ethos of military action, or the variety of sexual desire and practice, or specific religious beliefs and observances. Social distinctions and discrimination that are reflected in the plays are rarely taken into account, and when they are, carry the emphases of Bradley's time rather than those of Shakespeare's time or our own. These omissions are a principal reason why Bradley's strengths as a critic are less noticed and respected than they deserve at the present time. A reader aware of these further perspectives will find *Shakespearean Tragedy* to be wanting as a final assessment of Shakespeare's achievement but, nevertheless, if given a patient hearing, his book continues to offer a penetrating view of text and performance as they awaken many issues of morality, philosophy, psychology, individual identity, and intellectual understanding.

Bradley's criticism reaches those parts of a play that underlie the dialogue, and help a reader to understand why it was written in the way that Shakespeare chose. In consequence, *Shakespearean Tragedy* can help us to understand the open and performative nature of the texts. We begin to see why the tragedies continue to puzzle attentive readers and draw out the best in our most gifted and adventurous actors. In our minds, the insights of this book open up an inwardly motivated representation of exceptional lived experience. In a detailed and very practical way it can show an actor how Shakespeare's words may be used so that the lives of persons in a play seem grounded in fresh and individual sensations. For present-day critics, this book provides many examples of the risks involved in taking any statement in the plays concerning personal, political or social issues at its non-theatrical and purely verbal value. For all his obvious shortcomings, Bradley demonstrates, many times over, that the subtextual, physical, and interactive elements of performance are a significant part of Shakespeare's achievement. A critic who neglects that part will lose credibility among readers and audiences who follow the plays with what Bradley called eager minds and imagination.

CHAPTER SEVEN

Bradley's Scepticism and Search for a 'Tragic Vision'

Passages already quoted show that *Shakespearean Tragedy* advances some conclusions strongly and confidently, but this is not always so. Bradley wanted to explain every detail of the texts but distrusted his conclusions. In a 'Note' written for the second and later impressions he confessed:

■ I have confined myself to making some formal improvements, correcting indubitable mistakes, and indicating here and there my desire to modify or develop at some future time statements which seem to me doubtful or open to misunderstanding. The changes, where it seemed desirable, are shown by the inclusion of sentences in square brackets.   (p. viii) □

One of these parenthetical corrections (omitted in the 4th edition) – 'This paragraph states my view imperfectly' – comes after arguing that Hamlet never mentions his love for Ophelia in soliloquy because 'Shakespeare wrote primarily for the theatre and not for students' (p. 116). Bradley knew from experience that 'scarcely any spectators or readers of *Hamlet* notice this silence at all' but he could not be sure that Shakespeare had foreseen this or taken it into account (p. 116).

As he studied the words of a text and how they can come alive in imagination or performance, he was interested in much more than incidental issues. He also set out to describe 'Shakespeare's tragic vision', a view of human life that could confront the miseries, cruelties, and injustices of the world. Years before writing the book, Bradley had lost faith in the Christian God as a being superior to all others, the creator of the universe who had existed from the beginning of time and governed all things for the good of mankind and the salvation of souls. Like many other thinking men and women of his time, he still craved an alternative and reasonable faith in a superior being, and had come to believe that Shakespeare offered a route to that goal. Among much else, his book is an account of this quest.

'However great they may be and however decisive their actions may appear', Bradley noted that the heroes and heroines of Shakespeare's tragedies were very evidently not 'the ultimate power' in their world and was left asking what that might be: 'What account can we give of this world which will correspond with the imaginative impressions we receive' when reading or seeing the plays? (p. 15). He wanted to know who or what did govern human life and was responsible for the good and the bad.

As he engaged in this quest, he recognized three difficulties:

■ Most people, even among those who know Shakespeare well and come into real contact with his mind, are inclined to isolate and exaggerate some one aspect of the tragic fact. Some are so much influenced by their own habitual beliefs that they import them more or less into their interpretation of every author who is 'sympathetic' to them. And even where neither of these causes of error appears to operate, another is present from which it is probably impossible wholly to escape. . . . Any answer we give to the question proposed ought to correspond with, or to represent in terms of the understanding, our imaginative and emotional experience in reading the tragedies. . . . Yet it is extremely hard to make out exactly what this experience is, because, in the very effort to make it out, our reflecting mind, full of everyday ideas, is always tending to transform it by the application of these ideas, and so to elicit a result which, instead of representing the fact, conventionalizes it. And the consequence is not only mistaken theories; it is that many a man will declare that he feels in reading a tragedy what he never really felt, while he fails to recognize what he actually did feel. It is not likely that we shall escape all these dangers in our effort to find an answer to the question regarding the tragic world and the ultimate power in it.   (p. 15) □

Bradley knew that he was liable to be 'much influenced by [his] own habitual beliefs' and so gave his reasons for refusing any answer that was expressed 'in "religious" language':

■ For although this or that *dramatis personæ* may speak of gods or of God, of evil spirits or of Satan, of heaven and of hell, and although the poet may show us ghosts from another world, these ideas do not materially influence his representation of life, nor are they used to throw light on the mystery of its tragedy. The Elizabethan drama was almost wholly secular; and while Shakespeare was writing he practically confined his view to the world of non-theological observation and thought, so that he represents it substantially in one and the same way whether the period of the story is pre-Christian or Christian. He looked at this 'secular' world most intently and seriously; and he painted it, we cannot but conclude, with entire fidelity.   (p. 16) □

Discounting Christian or any other 'religious' answer to his question, Bradley propounded an impersonal influence in the affairs of men and women that operated without regard for good or evil and whether that guidance was heeded or not. By this means he explained how the tragedies seemed to move, as if by necessity, towards their conclusions and how the terrible events portrayed left readers and audiences with hope rather than despair. This force was not, he insisted, an implacable, disinterested fate; nor did it take responsibility away from individual human beings:

■ Whatever may be said of accidents, circumstances and the like, human action is, after all, presented to us as the central fact in tragedy, and also as the main cause of the catastrophe. That necessity which so much impresses us is, after all, chiefly the necessary connection of actions and consequences. For these actions we, without even raising a question on the subject, hold the agents responsible; and the tragedy would disappear for us if we did not. The critical action is, in greater or less degree, wrong or bad. The catastrophe is, in the main, the return of this action on the head of the agent. It is an example of justice; and that order which, present alike within the agents and outside them, infallibly brings it about, is therefore just. The rigour of its justice is terrible, no doubt, for a tragedy is a terrible story; but, in spite of fear and pity, we acquiesce, because our sense of justice is satisfied.   (p. 20) □

Having argued for the moral basis of tragedy, Bradley immediately interposed to insist that this did not involve what is usually termed 'poetic justice', a narrative that rewards and punishes in proportion to merit, both good and bad. That, says Bradley, would be 'in flagrant contradiction with the facts of life'. With regard to Shakespeare's tragedies:

■ I venture to say that it is a mistake to use at all these terms of justice and merit or desert. And this for two reasons. In the first place, essential as it is to recognize the connection between act and consequence, and natural as it may seem in some cases (*e.g.* Macbeth's) to say that the doer only gets what he deserves, yet in very many cases to say this would be quite unnatural. We might not object to the statement that Lear deserved to suffer for his folly, selfishness and tyranny; but to assert that he deserved to suffer what he did suffer is to do violence not merely to language but to any healthy moral sense. It is, moreover, to obscure the tragic fact that the consequences of action cannot be limited to that which would appear to us to follow 'justly' from them. . . .

But, in the second place, the ideas of justice and desert are, it seems to me, in *all* cases – even those of Richard III and of Macbeth and Lady Macbeth – untrue to our imaginative experience. When we are immersed in a tragedy, we feel towards dispositions, actions, and persons such emotions as attraction and repulsion, pity, wonder, fear, horror, perhaps hatred; but we do not *judge*. This is a point of view which emerges only when, in reading a play, we slip, by our own fault or the dramatist's, from the tragic position, or when, in thinking about the play afterwards, we fall back on our everyday legal and moral notions. But tragedy does not belong, any more than religion belongs, to the sphere of these notions; neither does the imaginative attitude in presence of it. While we are in its world we watch what is, seeing that so it happened and must have happened, feeling that it is piteous, dreadful, awful, mysterious, but neither passing sentence on the agents, nor asking whether the behaviour of the ultimate power towards them is just. And, therefore, the use of such language in attempts to render our imaginative experience in terms of the understanding is, to say the least, full of danger.   (pp. 21–2) □

Bradley was well aware of the difficult ground on which his argument rests. Mindful perhaps of Paulina in *The Winter's Tale* (V.iii.94–5), he tells his readers to 'awake [their] faith' in some power, greater than men and women, that manages their existence, however vaguely that power is located and identified:

■ when we call the order of the tragic world just, we are either using the word in some vague and unexplained sense, or we are going beyond what is shown us of this order, and are appealing to faith.   (p. 21) □

Bradley found that Shakespeare's 'tragic vision' is never verbally defined in the plays nor is it demonstrated in any one action: he could only point to the way they are structured or 'ordered' and attempt, again and again, to describe the assurance they brought.

Caught between a desire to have 'faith' in some greater than human power, and awe at the 'greatness' of heroes and heroines and the seeming necessity of their fate, Bradley gives almost no attention to the force of history or the influence of social and communal pressures. His view of the tragedies and his role as critic are adversely affected by these omissions but recognition of those limitations does nothing to lessen the effect of his uniquely penetrating enquiry into the sources and outcome of the thoughts and actions of the leading persons of these plays. Indeed Bradley's very limitations serve to throw into relief and heighten the effect of what his studies discovered. For most spectators and readers, individual actions and sensations hold the focus of attention during the last moments of the tragedies and these Bradley continues to illuminate. This is especially true when star actors are employed for then only a strong and imaginative director, with the help of stage and costume designers, can bring the wider interests of the tragedies into comparable prominence. Most readers will have to attend to historically learned and politically aware critics to gain a similar understanding of all that the plays portray.

At some points, and especially when considering the conclusion of *King Lear*, Bradley looked beyond the fate of a single tragic hero:

■ He is, in some way which we do not seek to define, untouched by the doom that overtakes him; and is rather set free from life than deprived of it. Some such feeling as this – some feeling which, from this description of it, may be recognized as their own even by those who would dissent from the description – we surely have in various degrees at the deaths of Hamlet and Othello and Lear, and of Antony and Cleopatra and Coriolanus. It accompanies the more prominent tragic impressions, and, regarded alone, could hardly be called tragic. For it seems to imply (though we are probably quite unconscious of the implication) an idea which, if developed, would transform the tragic view of things. It implies that the tragic world, if taken as it is presented, with all its error, guilt, failure, woe and waste, is no final reality, but only a part of reality taken for the whole, and, when so taken, illusive; and that if we could see the whole, and the tragic facts in their true place in it, we should find them, not abolished, of course, but so transmuted that they had ceased to be strictly tragic – find, perhaps, the suffering and death counting for little or nothing, the greatness of the soul for much or all, and the heroic spirit, in spite of failure, nearer to the heart of things than the smaller, more circumspect, and perhaps even 'better' beings who survived the catastrophe. The feeling which I have tried to describe, as accompanying the more obvious tragic emotions at the deaths of heroes, corresponds with some such idea as this.   (pp. 246–7) □

Bradley's scepticism ran deep and led him to think beyond theme, character, action, cause, and effect. For him, tragedies were not only stories about great men but also processes that provide an audience or reader with a perception that develops slowly through an imaginative response to a play in performance. The tragedies could only be defined in terms of the progressive experience they provide and a final clarification that is not stated in words but transcends them. Often the end result is not consciously comprehended but, nevertheless, is lasting in effect. In this his criticism is in keeping with the present times for these are parameters appropriate for responding to the plays of Beckett and Pinter, and the work of many other writers and artists today. Written a hundred years ago, Bradley's *Shakespearean Tragedy* is consonant with contemporary scepticism and the relativity of all understanding.

Our reception of the tragedies will be different from Bradley's but he shows us the nature of the experience they offer and the means by which they hold our attention to the very end. Shakespeare wrote no words that can sum up the final effect of his tragedies but, through the words, actions, and structure of the entire plays that Bradley so carefully examined with regard to their leading characters, we become aware of an understanding or sensation that seems to grow to 'great constancy' and may affect our view of the present-day world.

PART II

From *Shakespearean Tragedy* and later lectures

CHAPTER EIGHT

Hamlet

*T*he first of two Lectures on Hamlet is headed 'Shakespeare's Tragic Period –
Hamlet', and considers how Shakespeare's exceptional handling of narrative and
structure directs attention to Hamlet's inner consciousness by raising questions in the
audience's mind as the play evolves. Characteristically, Bradley closely examines both
words and action, dialogue and plotting.

■ Suppose you were to describe the plot of *Hamlet* to a person quite
ignorant of the play, and suppose you were careful to tell your hearer
nothing about Hamlet's character, what impression would your sketch
make on him? Would he not exclaim: 'What a sensational story! Why,
here are some eight violent deaths, not to speak of adultery, a ghost,
a mad woman, and a fight in a grave! If I did not know that the play
was Shakespeare's, I should have thought it must have been one of
those early tragedies of blood and horror from which he is said to have
redeemed the stage'? And would he not then go on to ask: 'But why
in the world did not Hamlet obey the Ghost at once, and so save seven
of those eight lives?'

The exclamation and this question both show the same thing, that
the whole story turns upon the peculiar character of the hero. For
without this character the story would appear sensational and horrible;
and yet the actual *Hamlet* is very far from being so, and even has a less
terrible effect than *Othello*, *King Lear* or *Macbeth*. And again, if we had
no knowledge of this character, the story would hardly be intelligible;
it would at any rate at once suggest that wondering question about the
conduct of the hero; while the story of any of the other three tragedies
would sound plain enough and would raise no such question. It is
further very probable that the main change made by Shakespeare in
the story as already represented on the stage, lay in a new conception
of Hamlet's character and so of the cause of his delay. And, lastly,
when we examine the tragedy, we observe two things which illustrate

the same point. First, we find by the side of the hero no other figure of tragic proportions, no one like Lady Macbeth or Iago, no one even like Cordelia or Desdemona; so that, in Hamlet's absence, the remaining characters could not yield a Shakespearean tragedy at all. And, secondly, we find among them two, Laertes and Fortinbras, who are evidently designed to throw the character of the hero into relief. Even in the situations there is a curious parallelism; for Fortinbras, like Hamlet, is the son of a king, lately dead, and succeeded by his brother; and Laertes, like Hamlet, has a father slain, and feels bound to avenge him. And with this parallelism in situation there is a strong contrast in character; for both Fortinbras and Laertes possess in abundance the very quality which the hero seems to lack, so that, as we read, we are tempted to exclaim that either of them would have accomplished Hamlet's task in a day. Naturally, then, the tragedy of *Hamlet* with Hamlet left out has become the symbol of extreme absurdity; while the character itself has probably exerted a greater fascination, and certainly has been the subject of more discussion, than any other in the whole literature of the world.   (pp. 64–5) □

Having established why questions are asked, Bradley has little but scorn for the last two answers he considers:

■ We come next to what may be called the sentimental view of Hamlet, a view common both among his worshippers and among his defamers. Its germ may perhaps be found in an unfortunate phrase of Goethe's (who of course is not responsible for the whole view): 'a lovely, pure and most moral nature, *without the strength of nerve which forms a hero*, sinks beneath a burden which it cannot bear and must not cast away' [*Wilhelm Meister*, 1795]. When this idea is isolated, developed and popularized, we get the picture of a graceful youth, sweet and sensitive, full of delicate sympathies and yearning aspirations, shrinking from the touch of everything gross and earthly; but frail and weak. . . . But for the 'sentimental' Hamlet you can feel only pity not unmingled with contempt. Whatever else he is, he is no *hero*.

But consider the text. This shrinking, flower-like youth – how could he possibly have done what we *see* Hamlet do? What likeness to him is there in the Hamlet who, summoned by the Ghost, bursts from his terrified friends with the cry:

> Unhand me, gentlemen!
> By heaven, I'll make a ghost of him that lets me;

the Hamlet who scarcely once speaks to the King without an insult, or to Polonius without a gibe; the Hamlet who storms at Ophelia and speaks daggers to his mother; the Hamlet who, hearing a cry behind the arras, whips out his sword in an instant and runs the eavesdropper through; the Hamlet who sends his 'school-fellows' to their death and never troubles his head about them more; the Hamlet who is the first man to board a pirate ship, and who fights with Laertes in the grave; the Hamlet of the catastrophe, an omnipotent fate, before whom all the court stands helpless, who, as the truth breaks upon him, rushes on the King, drives his foil right through his body, then seizes the poisoned cup and forces it violently between the wretched man's lips, and in the throes of death has force and fire enough to wrest the cup from Horatio's hand ('By heaven, I'll have it!') lest he should drink and die? This man, the Hamlet of the play, is a heroic, terrible figure. He would have been formidable to Othello or Macbeth. If the senti-mental Hamlet had crossed him, he would have hurled him from his path with one sweep of his arm.

This view, then, or any view that approaches it, is grossly unjust to Hamlet, and turns tragedy into mere pathos. But, on the other side, it is too kind to him. It ignores the hardness and cynicism which were indeed no part of his nature, but yet, in this crisis of his life, are indu-bitably present and painfully marked. His sternness, itself left out of sight by this theory, is no defect; but he is much more than stern. Polonius possibly deserved nothing better than the words addressed to his corpse:

Thou wretched, rash, intruding fool, farewell!
I took thee for thy better: take thy fortune:
Thou find'st to be too busy is some danger;

yet this was Ophelia's father, and, whatever he deserved, it pains us, for Hamlet's sake, to hear the words:

This man shall set me packing:
I'll lug the guts into the neighbour room.

There is the same insensibility in Hamlet's language about the fate of Rosencrantz and Guildenstern; and, observe, their deaths were not in the least required by his purpose. Grant, again, that his cruelty to Ophelia was partly due to misunderstanding, partly forced on him, partly feigned; still one surely cannot altogether so account for it, and still less can one so account for the disgusting and insulting grossness of his language to her in the play-scene. I know this is said to be merely an example of the custom of Shakespeare's time. But it is not so. It is such language as you will find addressed to a woman by no other hero of Shakespeare's, not even in that dreadful scene where

45

Othello accuses Desdemona. It is a great mistake to ignore these things, or to try to soften the impression which they naturally make on one. That this embitterment, callousness, grossness, brutality, should be induced on a soul so pure and noble is profoundly tragic; and Shakespeare's business was to show this tragedy, not to paint an ideally beautiful soul unstained and undisturbed by the evil of the world and the anguish of conscious failure.

There remains, finally, that class of view which may be named after Schlegel and Coleridge. According to this, *Hamlet* is the tragedy of reflection. The cause of the hero's delay is irresolution; and the cause of this irresolution is excess of the reflective or speculative habit of mind. He has a general intention to obey the Ghost, but 'the native hue of resolution is sicklied o'er with the pale cast of thought'. He is 'thought-sick'. 'The whole', says Schlegel, 'is intended to show how a calculating consideration which aims at exhausting, so far as human foresight can, all the relations and possible consequences of a deed, cripples the power of acting. ... Hamlet is a hypocrite towards himself; his far-fetched scruples are often mere pretexts to cover his want of determination. ... He has no firm belief in himself or in anything else. ... He loses himself in labyrinths of thought.' So Coleridge finds in Hamlet 'an almost enormous intellectual activity and a proportionate aversion to real action consequent upon it' (the aversion, that is to say, is consequent on the activity). ...

We come at last into close contact with the text of the play. It not only answers, in some fundamental respects, to the general impression produced by the drama, but it can be supported by Hamlet's own words in his soliloquies – such words, for example, as those about the native hue of resolution, or those about the craven scruple of thinking too precisely on the event. It is confirmed, also, by the contrast between Hamlet on the one side, and Laertes and Fortinbras on the other; and, further, by the occurrence of those words of the King to Laertes (IV.vii.119f.), which, if they are not in character, are all the more important as showing what was in Shakespeare's mind at the time:

> that we would do
> We should do when we would; for this 'would' changes,
> And hath abatements and delays as many
> As there are tongues, are hands, are accidents;
> And then this 'should' is like a spendthrift sigh
> That hurts by easing.

And, lastly, even if the view itself does not suffice, the *description* given by its adherents of Hamlet's state of mind, as we see him in the last four Acts, is, on the whole and so far as it goes, a true description. The energy of resolve is dissipated in an endless brooding on the deed required. When he acts, his action does not proceed from this deliberation and analysis, but is sudden and impulsive, evoked by an emergency in which he has no time to think. And most of the reasons he assigns for his procrastination are evidently not the true reasons, but unconscious excuses.

Nevertheless this theory fails to satisfy. And it fails not merely in this or that detail, but as a whole. We feel that its Hamlet does not fully answer to our imaginative impression. He is not nearly so inadequate to this impression as the sentimental Hamlet, but still we feel he is inferior to Shakespeare's man and does him wrong. . . . Hamlet's irresolution, or his aversion to real action, is, according to the theory, the *direct* result of 'an almost enormous intellectual activity' in the way of 'a calculating consideration which attempts to exhaust all the relations and possible consequences of a deed'. And this again proceeds from an original one-sidedness of nature, strengthened by habit, and, perhaps, by years of speculative inaction. The theory describes, therefore, a man in certain respects like Coleridge himself, on one side a man of genius, on the other side, the side of will, deplorably weak, always procrastinating and avoiding unpleasant duties, and often reproaching himself in vain; a man, observe, who at *any* time and in *any* circumstances would be unequal to the task assigned to Hamlet. And thus, I must maintain, it degrades Hamlet and travesties the play. For Hamlet, according to all the indications in the text, was not naturally or normally such a man, but rather, I venture to affirm, a man who at any *other* time and in any *other* circumstances than those presented would have been perfectly equal to his task; and it is, in fact, the very cruelty of his fate that the crisis of his life comes on him at the one moment when he cannot meet it, and when his highest gifts, instead of helping him, conspire to paralyse him. This aspect of the tragedy the theory quite misses; and it does so because it misconceives the cause of that irresolution which, on the whole, it truly describes. For the cause was not directly or mainly an habitual excess of reflectiveness. The direct cause was a state of mind quite abnormal and induced by special circumstances – a state of profound melancholy. Now, Hamlet's reflectiveness doubtless played a certain part in the *production* of that melancholy, and was thus one indirect contributory cause of his irresolution. And, again, the melancholy, once established, displayed, as one of its *symptoms*, an excessive reflection on the required deed. But excess of reflection was not, as the theory makes it, the *direct* cause of the irresolution at all; nor was it the *only* indirect cause; and in the Hamlet of the last four Acts it is to be considered rather a symptom of his state than a cause of it.   (pp. 73–8) □

Having noted the importance of Hamlet's melancholy, Bradley considers several explanations of an inherent 'danger' in his nature and, quoting 'What a piece of work is a man!' (II.ii.305–6), concludes by blaming an idealism that is seen in his attraction to the 'good' and revulsion from the 'bad'. He locates these feelings in Hamlet's 'soul', which implies that they are instinctive and central to his nature.

■ Where else in Shakespeare is there anything like Hamlet's adoration of his father? The words melt into music whenever he speaks of him. And, if there are no signs of any such feeling towards his mother, though many signs of love, it is characteristic that he evidently never entertained a suspicion of anything unworthy in her – characteristic, and significant of his tendency to see only what is good unless he is forced to see the reverse. For we find this tendency elsewhere, and find it going so far that we must call it a disposition to idealize, to see something better than what is there, or at least to ignore deficiencies. He says to Laertes, 'I loved you ever', and he describes Laertes as a 'very noble youth', which he was far from being. In his first greeting of Rosencrantz and Guildenstern, where his old self revives, we trace the same affectionateness and readiness to take men at their best. His love for Ophelia, too, which seems strange to some, is surely the most natural thing in the world. He saw her innocence, simplicity and sweetness, and it was like him to ask no more; and it is noticeable that Horatio, though entirely worthy of his friendship, is, like Ophelia, intellectually not remarkable. To the very end, however clouded, this generous disposition, this 'free and open nature', this unsuspiciousness survive. They cost him his life; for the King knew them, and was sure that he was too 'generous and free from all contriving' to 'peruse the foils'. To the very end, his soul, however sick and tortured it may be, answers instantaneously when good and evil are presented to it, loving the one and hating the other. He is called a sceptic who has no firm belief in anything, but he is never sceptical about *them*.

And the negative side of his idealism, the aversion to evil, is perhaps even more developed in the hero of the tragedy than in the Hamlet of earlier days. It is intensely characteristic. Nothing, I believe, is to be found elsewhere in Shakespeare (unless in the rage of the disillusioned idealist Timon) of quite the same kind as Hamlet's disgust at his uncle's drunkenness, his loathing of his mother's sensuality, his astonishment and horror at her shallowness, his contempt for everything pretentious or false, his indifference to everything merely external. This last characteristic appears in his choice of the friend of his heart, and in a certain impatience of distinctions of rank or wealth. When Horatio calls his father 'a goodly king', he answers, surely with an emphasis on 'man',

He was a man, take him for all in all,
I shall not look upon his like again.

He will not listen to talk of Horatio being his 'servant'. When the others speak of their 'duty' to him, he answers, 'Your love, as mine to you'. He speaks to the actor precisely as he does to an honest courtier. He is not in the least a revolutionary, but still, in effect, a king and a beggar are all one to him. He cares for nothing but human worth, and his pitilessness towards Polonius and Osric and his 'school-fellows' is not wholly due to morbidity, but belongs in part to his original character.

Now, in Hamlet's moral sensibility there undoubtedly lay a danger. Any great shock that life might inflict on it would be felt with extreme intensity. Such a shock might even produce tragic results. And, in fact, *Hamlet* deserves the title 'tragedy of moral idealism' quite as much as the title 'tragedy of reflection'.

With this temperament and this sensibility we find, lastly, in the Hamlet of earlier days, as of later, intellectual genius. It is chiefly this that makes him so different from all those about him, good and bad alike, and hardly less different from most of Shakespeare's other heroes. And this, though on the whole the most important trait in his nature, is also so obvious and so famous that I need not dwell on it at length. But against one prevalent misconception I must say a word of warning. Hamlet's intellectual power is not a specific gift, like a genius for music or mathematics or philosophy. It shows itself, fitfully, in the affairs of life as unusual quickness of perception, great agility in shifting the mental attitude, a striking rapidity and fertility in resource; so that, when his natural belief in others does not make him unwary, Hamlet easily sees through them and masters them, and no one can be much less like the typical helpless dreamer. It shows itself in conversation chiefly in the form of wit or humour; and, alike in conversation and in soliloquy, it shows itself in the form of imagination quite as much as in that of thought in the stricter sense. . . .

Hamlet had speculative genius without being a philosopher, just as he had imaginative genius without being a poet. Doubtless in happier days he was a close and constant observer of men and manners, noting his results in those tables which he afterwards snatched from his breast to make in wild irony his last note of all, that one may smile and smile and be a villain. Again and again we remark that passion for generalization which so occupied him, for instance, in reflections suggested by the King's drunkenness that he quite forgot what it was he was waiting to meet upon the battlements. Doubtless, too, he was always considering things, as Horatio thought, too curiously. There was a necessity in his soul driving him to penetrate below the surface and to question what others took for granted. That fixed habitual look which the world wears for most men did not exist for him. He was for ever unmaking his world and rebuilding it in thought, dissolving what to others were solid facts, and discovering what to others were old truths. There were no old truths for Hamlet. It is for Horatio a thing of course that there's a divinity that shapes our ends, but for Hamlet it is a discovery hardly won. And throughout this kingdom of the mind, where he felt that man, who in action is only like an angel, is in apprehension like a god, he moved (we must imagine) more than content, so that even in his dark days he declares he could be bounded in a nutshell and yet count himself a king of infinite space, were it not that he had bad dreams.

If now we ask whether any special danger lurked *here*, how shall we answer? . . . Turn to the first words Hamlet utters when he is alone; turn, that is to say, to the place where the author is likely to indicate his meaning most plainly. What do you hear?

> O, that this too too solid flesh would melt,
> Thaw and resolve itself into a dew!
> Or that the Everlasting had not fix'd
> His canon 'gainst self-slaughter! O God! God!
> How weary, stale, flat and unprofitable,
> Seem to me all the uses of this world!
> Fie on't! ah fie! 'tis an unweeded garden,
> That grows to seed; things rank and gross in nature
> Possess it merely.

Here are a sickness of life, and even a longing for death, so intense that nothing stands between Hamlet and suicide except religious awe. And what has caused them? The rest of the soliloquy so thrusts the answer upon us that it might seem impossible to miss it. It was not his father's death; that doubtless brought deep grief, but mere grief for some one loved and lost does not make a noble spirit loathe the world as a place full only of things rank and gross. It was not the vague suspicion that we know Hamlet felt. Still less was it the loss of the crown; for though the subserviency of the electors might well disgust him, there is not a reference to the subject in the soliloquy, nor any sign elsewhere that it greatly occupied his mind. It was the moral shock of the sudden ghastly disclosure of his mother's true nature, falling on him when his heart was aching with love, and his body doubtless was weakened by sorrow. And it is essential, however disagreeable, to realize the nature of this shock. It matters little here whether Hamlet's age was twenty or thirty: in either case his mother was a matron of mature years. All his life he had believed in her, we may be sure, as such a son would. He had seen her not merely devoted to his father, but hanging on him like a newly-wedded bride, hanging on him

As if increase of appetite had grown
By what it fed on.

He had seen her following his body 'like Niobe, all tears'. And then within a month – 'O God! a beast would have mourned longer' – she married again, and married Hamlet's uncle, a man utterly contemptible and loathsome in his eyes; married him in what to Hamlet was inces-tuous wedlock;★ married him not for any reason of state, nor even out of old family affection, but in such a way that her son was forced to see in her action not only an astounding shallowness of feeling but an eruption of coarse sensuality, 'rank and gross', speeding post-haste to its horrible delight. Is it possible to conceive an experience more deso-lating to a man such as we have seen Hamlet to be; and is its result anything but perfectly natural? It brings bewildered horror, then loathing, then despair of human nature. His whole mind is poisoned. He can never see Ophelia in the same light again: she is a woman, and his mother is a woman: if she mentions the word 'brief' to him, the answer drops from his lips like venom, 'as woman's love'. The last words of the soliloquy, which is *wholly* concerned with this subject, are,

But, break, my heart, for I must hold my tongue!

He can do nothing. He must lock in his heart, not any suspicion of his uncle that moves obscurely there, but that horror and loathing; and if his heart ever found relief, it was when those feelings, mingled with the love that never died out in him, poured themselves forth in a flood as he stood in his mother's chamber beside his father's marriage-bed.

If we still wonder, and ask why the effect of this shock should be so tremendous, let us observe that *now* the conditions have arisen under which Hamlet's highest endowments, his moral sensibility and his genius, become his enemies. A nature morally blunter would have felt even so dreadful a revelation less keenly. A slower and more limited and positive mind might not have extended so widely through its world the disgust and disbelief that have entered it. But Hamlet has

---

★ This aspect of the matter leaves us comparatively unaffected, but Shakespeare evidently means it to be of importance. The Ghost speaks of it twice, and Hamlet thrice (once in his last furious words to the King). If, as we must suppose, the marriage was universally admitted to be incestuous, the corrupt acquiescence of the court and the electors to the crown would naturally have a strong effect on Hamlet's mind.

the imagination which, for evil as well as good, feels and sees all things in one. Thought is the element of his life, and his thought is infected. He cannot prevent himself from probing and lacerating the wound in his soul. One idea, full of peril, holds him fast, and he cries out in agony at it, but is impotent to free himself ('Must I remember?' 'Let me not think on't'). And when, with the fading of his passion, the vividness of this idea abates, it does so only to leave behind a boundless weariness and a sick longing for death.

And this is the time which his fate chooses. In this hour of uttermost weakness, this sinking of his whole being towards annihilation, there comes on him, bursting the bounds of the natural world with a shock of astonishment and terror, the revelation of his mother's adultery and his father's murder, and, with this, the demand on him, in the name of everything dearest and most sacred, to arise and act. And for a moment, though his brain reels and totters, his soul leaps up in passion to answer this demand. But it comes too late. It does but strike home the last rivet in the melancholy which holds him bound.

> The time is out of joint! O cursed spite
> That ever I was born to set it right –

so he mutters within an hour of the moment when he vowed to give his life to the duty of revenge; and the rest of the story exhibits his vain efforts to fulfil this duty, his unconscious self-excuses and unavailing self-reproaches, and the tragic results of his delay. . . .

★　★　★

'Melancholy,' I said, not dejection, nor yet insanity. That Hamlet was not far from insanity is very probable. His adoption of the pretence of madness may well have been due in part to fear of the reality; to an instinct of self-preservation, a fore-feeling that the pretence would enable him to give some utterance to the load that pressed on his heart and brain, and a fear that he would be unable altogether to repress such utterance. And if the pathologist calls his state melancholia, and even proceeds to determine its species, I see nothing to object to in that; I am grateful to him for emphasizing the fact that Hamlet's melancholy was no mere common depression of spirits; and I have no doubt that many readers of the play would understand it better if they read an account of melancholia in a work on mental diseases. If we like to use the word 'disease' loosely, Hamlet's condition may truly be called diseased. No exertion of will could have dispelled it. Even if he had been able at once to do the bidding of the Ghost he would doubtless have still remained for some time under the cloud. It would be absurdly unjust to call *Hamlet* a study of melancholy, but it contains such a study.

But this melancholy is something very different from insanity, in anything like the usual meaning of that word. No doubt it might develop into insanity. The longing for death might become an irresistible impulse to self-destruction; the disorder of feeling and will might extend to sense and intellect; delusions might arise; and the man might become, as we say, incapable and irresponsible. But Hamlet's melancholy is some way from this condition. It is a totally different thing from the madness which he feigns; and he never, when alone or in company with Horatio alone, exhibits the signs of that madness. Nor is the dramatic use of this melancholy, again, open to the objections which would justly be made to the portrayal of an insanity which brought the hero to a tragic end. The man who suffers as Hamlet suffers – and thousands go about their business suffering thus in greater or less degree – is considered irresponsible neither by other people nor by himself: he is only too keenly conscious of his responsibility. He is therefore, so far, quite capable of being a tragic agent, which an insane person, at any rate according to Shakespeare's practice, is not. . . .

This state [of mind] accounts for Hamlet's energy as well as for his lassitude, those quick decided actions of his being the outcome of a nature normally far from passive, now suddenly stimulated, and producing healthy impulses which work themselves out before they have time to subside. It accounts for the evidently keen satisfaction which some of these actions give to him. He arranges the play-scene with lively interest, and exults in its success, not really because it brings him nearer to his goal, but partly because it has hurt his enemy and partly because it has demonstrated his own skill (III.ii.286–304). He looks forward almost with glee to countermining the King's designs in sending him away (III.iv.209), and looks back with obvious satisfaction, even with pride, to the address and vigour he displayed on the voyage (V.ii.1–55). These were not *the* action on which his morbid self-feeling had centred; he feels in them his old force, and escapes in them from his disgust. It accounts for the pleasure with which he meets old acquaintances, like his 'school-fellows' or the actors. The former observed (and we can observe) in him a 'kind of joy' at first, though it is followed by 'much forcing of his disposition' as he attempts to keep his joy and his courtesy alive in spite of the misery which so soon returns upon him and the suspicion he is forced to feel. It accounts no less for the painful features of his character as seen in the play, his almost savage irritability on the one hand, and on the other his self-absorption, his callousness, his insensibility to the fates of those whom he despises, and to the feelings even of those whom he loves. These are frequent symptoms of such melancholy, and they sometimes alternate, as they do in Hamlet, with bursts of transitory, almost hysterical, and quite fruitless emotion. It is to these last (of which a part of the soliloquy, 'O what a rogue', gives a good example) that Hamlet alludes when, to the Ghost, he speaks of himself as 'lapsed in *passion*', and it is doubtless partly his conscious weakness in regard to them that inspires his praise of Horatio as a man who is not 'passion's slave'.

Finally, Hamlet's melancholy accounts for two things which seem to be explained by nothing else. The first of these is his apathy or 'lethargy'. We are bound to consider the evidence which the text supplies of this, though it is usual to ignore it. When Hamlet mentions, as one possible cause of his inaction, his 'thinking too precisely on the event', he mentions another, 'bestial oblivion'; and the thing against which he inveighs in the greater part of that soliloquy (IV.iv.) is not the excess or the misuse of reason (which for him here and always is god-like), but this *bestial* oblivion or '*dullness*', this 'letting all *sleep*', this allowing of heaven-sent reason to 'fust unused':

> What is a man,
> If his chief good and market of his time
> Be but to *sleep* and feed? a *beast*, no more.

So, in the soliloquy in II.ii. he accuses himself of being 'a *dull* and muddy-mettled rascal', who 'peaks [mopes] like John-a-dreams, unpregnant of his cause', dully indifferent to his cause. So, when the Ghost appears to him the second time, he accuses himself of being tardy and lapsed in *time*; and the Ghost speaks of his purpose being almost *blunted*, and bids him not to *forget* (cf. 'oblivion'). And so, what is emphasized in those undramatic but significant speeches of the player-king and of Claudius is the mere dying away of purpose or of love [see III.ii.196ff., IV.vii.111ff.]. Surely what all this points to is not a condition of excessive but useless mental activity (indeed there is, in reality, curiously little about that in the text), but rather one of dull, apathetic, brooding gloom, in which Hamlet, so far from analysing his duty, is not thinking of it at all, but for the time literally *forgets* it. It seems to me we are driven to think of Hamlet *chiefly* thus during the long time which elapsed between the appearance of the Ghost and the events presented in the Second Act. The Ghost, in fact, had more reason than we suppose at first for leaving with Hamlet as his parting injunction the command, 'Remember me', and for greeting him, on reappearing, with the command, 'Do not forget'. These little things in Shakespeare are not accidents.

The second trait which is fully explained only by Hamlet's melancholy is his own inability to understand why he delays. This emerges in a marked degree when an occasion like the player's emotion or the sight of Fortinbras's army stings Hamlet into shame at his inaction. '*Why*,' he asks himself in genuine bewilderment, 'do I linger? Can the cause be cowardice? Can it be sloth? Can it be thinking too precisely of the event? And does *that* again mean cowardice? What is it that makes me sit idle when I feel it is shameful to do so, and when I have *cause, and will, and strength, and means* to act?' A man irresolute merely because he was considering a proposed action too minutely would not feel this bewilderment. A man might feel it whose conscience secretly condemned the act which his explicit consciousness approved; but we have seen that there is no sufficient evidence to justify us in conceiving Hamlet thus. These are the questions of a man stimulated for the moment to shake off the weight of his melancholy, and, because for the moment he is free from it, unable to understand the paralysing pressure which it exerts at other times.

I have dwelt thus at length on Hamlet's melancholy because, from the psychological point of view, it is the centre of the tragedy, and to omit it from consideration or to underrate its intensity is to make Shakespeare's story unintelligible. But the psychological point of view is not equivalent to the tragic; and, having once given its due weight to the fact of Hamlet's melancholy, we may freely admit, or rather may be anxious to insist, that this pathological condition would excite but little, if any, tragic interest if it were not the condition of a nature distinguished by that speculative genius on which the Schlegel–Coleridge type of theory lays stress. Such theories misinterpret the connection between that genius and Hamlet's failure, but still it is this connection which gives to his story its peculiar fascination and makes it appear (if the phrase may be allowed) as the symbol of a tragic mystery inherent in human nature. Wherever this mystery touches us, wherever we are forced to feel the wonder and awe of man's godlike 'apprehension' and his 'thoughts that wander through eternity', and at the same time are forced to see him powerless in his petty sphere of action, and powerless (it would appear) from the very divinity of his thought, we remember Hamlet. And this is the reason why, in the great ideal movement which began towards the close of the eighteenth century, this tragedy acquired a position unique among Shakespeare's dramas, and shared only by Goethe's *Faust*. It was not that *Hamlet* is Shakespeare's greatest tragedy or most perfect work of art; it was that *Hamlet* most brings home to us at once the sense of the soul's infinity, and the sense of the doom which not only circumscribes that infinity but appears to be its offspring.   (pp. 80–93) □

Bradley's second Lecture on Hamlet *starts with an admission of doubt and then proposes a course of action that is typical of his close focus on the hero and his attention to detail*:

■ The only way, if there is any way, in which a conception of Hamlet's character could be proved true, would be to show that it, and it alone, explains all the relevant facts presented by the text of the drama. To attempt such a demonstration here would obviously be impossible, even if I felt certain of the interpretation of all the facts. But I propose now to follow rapidly the course of the action in so far as it specially illustrates the character, reserving for separate consideration one important but particularly doubtful point.   (p. 94) ☐

Having identified Hamlet's relationship to his mother as crucial to the tragedy, Bradley spends great care on the closet scene (Act III, scene iv), the one sustained scene between them. This is given in full here as representative of the lively account of the text that follows the diagnosis of Hamlet's melancholy. It also illustrates Bradley's habit of looking before and after when examining a highly dramatic or doubtful moment. As he gave warning, his reading of the text is not always 'certain' and will often raise conflicting responses. Present-day readers, actors and audiences are likely to find some of his interpretations sentimental and limited by his personal outlook but, at these times, his criticism can mark for us the extent to which Shakespeare's text has many levels of meaning.

■ The incident of the sparing of the King [Act II, scene ii] is contrived with extraordinary dramatic insight. On the one side we feel that the opportunity was perfect. Hamlet could not possibly any longer tell himself that he had no certainty as to his uncle's guilt. And the external conditions were most favourable; for the King's remarkable behaviour at the play-scene would have supplied a damning confirmation of the story Hamlet had to tell about the Ghost. Even now, probably, in a Court so corrupt as that of Elsinore, he could not with perfect security have begun by charging the King with the murder; but he could quite safely have killed him first and given his justification afterwards, especially as he would certainly have had on his side the people, who loved him and despised Claudius. On the other hand, Shakespeare has taken care to give this perfect opportunity so repulsive a character that we can hardly bring ourselves to wish that the hero should accept it. One of his minor difficulties, we have seen, probably was that he seemed to be required to attack a defenceless man: and here this difficulty is at its maximum.

This incident is, again, the turning-point of the tragedy. So far, Hamlet's delay, though it is endangering his freedom and his life, has done no irreparable harm; but his failure here is the cause of all the disasters that follow. In sparing the King, he sacrifices Polonius, Ophelia, Rosencrantz and Guildenstern, Laertes, the Queen and himself. This central significance of the passage is dramatically indicated in the following scene by the reappearance of the Ghost and the repetition of its charge.

Polonius is the first to fall. The old courtier, whose vanity would not allow him to confess that his diagnosis of Hamlet's lunacy was mistaken, had suggested that, after the theatricals, the Queen should endeavour in a private interview with her son to penetrate the mystery, while he himself would repeat his favourite part of eavesdropper (III.i.184ff.). It has now become quite imperative that the Prince should be brought to disclose his secret; for his choice of the 'Murder of Gonzago', and perhaps his conduct during the performance, have shown a spirit of exaggerated hostility against the King which has excited general alarm. Rosencrantz and Guildenstern discourse to Claudius on the extreme importance of his preserving his invaluable life, as though Hamlet's insanity had now clearly shown itself to be homicidal. When, then, at the opening of the interview between Hamlet and his mother, the son, instead of listening to her remonstrances, roughly assumes the offensive, she becomes alarmed; and when, on her attempting to leave the room, he takes her by the arm and forces her to sit down, she is terrified, cries out, 'Thou wilt not murder me?' and screams for help. Polonius, behind the arras, echoes her call; and in a moment Hamlet, hoping the concealed person is the King, runs the old man through the body.

Evidently this act is intended to stand in sharp contrast with Hamlet's sparing of his enemy. The King would have been just as defenceless behind the arras as he had been on his knees; but here Hamlet is already excited and in action, and the chance comes to him so suddenly that he has no time to 'scan' it. It is a minor consideration, but still for the dramatist not unimportant, that the audience would wholly sympathize with Hamlet's attempt here, as directed against an enemy who is lurking to entrap him, instead of being engaged in a business which perhaps to the bulk of the audience then, as now, seemed to have a 'relish of salvation in't'.

We notice in Hamlet, at the opening of this interview, something of the excited levity which followed the *dénouement* of the play-scene. The death of Polonius sobers him; and in the remainder of the interview he shows, together with some traces of his morbid state, the peculiar beauty and nobility of his nature. His chief desire is not by any means to ensure his mother's silent acquiescence in his design of revenge; it is to save her soul. And while the rough work of vengeance is repugnant to him, he is at home in this higher work. Here that fatal feeling, 'it is no matter', never shows itself. No father-confessor could be more selflessly set upon his end of redeeming a fellow-creature from degradation, more stern or pitiless in denouncing the sin, or more eager to welcome the first token of repentance. There is something infinitely beautiful in that sudden sunshine of faith and love which breaks out when, at the Queen's surrender,

> O Hamlet, thou has cleft my heart in twain,

he answers,

> O throw away the worser part of it,
> And live the purer with the other half.

The truth is that, though Hamlet hates his uncle and acknowledges the duty of vengeance, his whole heart is never in this feeling or this task; but his whole heart is in his horror at his mother's fall and in his longing to raise her. The former of these feelings was the inspiration of his first soliloquy; it combines with the second to form the inspiration of his eloquence here. And Shakespeare never wrote more eloquently than here.

I have already alluded to the significance of the reappearance of the Ghost in this scene; but why does Shakespeare choose for the particular moment of its reappearance the middle of a speech in which Hamlet is raving against his uncle? There seems to be more than one reason. In the first place, Hamlet has already attained his object of stirring shame and contrition in his mother's breast, and is now yielding to the old temptation of unpacking his heart with words, and exhausting in useless emotion the force which should be stored up in his will. And, next, in doing this he is agonizing his mother to no purpose, and in despite of her piteous and repeated appeals for mercy. But the Ghost, when it gave him his charge, had expressly warned him to spare her; and here again the dead husband shows the same tender regard for his weak unfaithful wife. The object of his return is to repeat his charge:

> Do not forget: this visitation
> Is but to whet thy almost blunted purpose;

but, having uttered the reminder, he immediately bids the son to help the mother and 'step between her and her fighting soul'.

And, whether intentionally or not, another purpose is served by Shakespeare's choice of this particular moment. It is a moment when the state of Hamlet's mind is such that we cannot suppose the Ghost to be meant for an hallucination; and it is of great importance here that the spectator or reader should not suppose any such thing. He is further guarded by the fact that the Ghost proves, so to speak, his identity by showing the same traits as were visible on his first appearance – the same insistence on the duty of remembering, and the same concern for the Queen. And the result is that we construe the Ghost's interpretation of Hamlet's delay ('almost blunted purpose') as the truth, the dramatist's own interpretation. Let me add that probably no one in Shakespeare's audience had any doubt of his meaning here. The idea of later critics and readers that the Ghost is an hallucination is due partly to failure to follow the indications just noticed, but partly also to two mistakes, the substitution of our present intellectual atmosphere for the Elizabethan, and the notion that, because the Queen does not see and hear the Ghost, it is meant to be unreal. But a ghost, in Shakespeare's day, was able for any sufficient reason to confine its manifestation to a single person in a company; and here the sufficient reason, that of sparing the Queen, is obvious.

At the close of this scene it appears that Hamlet has somehow learned of the King's design of sending him to England in charge of his two 'school-fellows'. He has no doubt that this design covers some villainous plot against himself, but neither does he doubt that he will succeed in defeating it; and, as we saw it, he looks forward with plea-sure to this conflict of wits. The idea of refusing to go appears not to occur to him. Perhaps (for here we are left to conjecture) he feels that he could not refuse unless at the same time he openly accused the King of his father's murder (a course which he seems at no time to contem-plate); for by the slaughter of Polonius he has supplied his enemy with the best possible excuse for getting him out of the country. Besides, he has so effectually warned this enemy, that after the death of Polonius is discovered, he is kept under guard (IV.iii.14). He consents, then, to go. But on his way to the shore he meets the army of Fortinbras on its march to Poland; and the sight of these men going cheerfully to risk death 'for an eggshell', and 'making mouths at the invisible event', strikes him with shame as he remembers how he, with so much greater cause for action, 'lets all sleep'; and he breaks out into the soliloquy, 'How all occasions do inform against me!'   (pp. 99–103) ☐

Bradley is at his most doubtful about Hamlet's relationship to Ophelia (see also p. 34, above):

■ The actor who plays the part of Hamlet must make up his mind as to the interpretation of every word and deed of the character. Even if at some point he feels no certainty as to which of two interpretations is right, he must still choose one or the other. The mere critic is not obliged to do this. Where he remains in doubt he may say so, and, if the matter is of importance, he ought to say so.

This is the position in which I find myself in regard to Hamlet's love for Ophelia. I am unable to arrive at a conviction as to the meaning of some of his words and deeds, and I question whether from the mere text of the play a sure interpretation of them can be drawn. . . . I suggest, first, that Hamlet's love, though never lost, was, after

Ophelia's apparent rejection of him, mingled with suspicion and resentment, and that his treatment of her was due in part to this cause. . . . But the question how much of his harshness is meant to be real, and how much assumed, seems to me impossible in some places to answer. For example, his behaviour at the play-scene seems to me to show an intention to hurt and insult; but in the Nunnery-scene (which cannot be discussed briefly) he is evidently acting a part and suffering acutely, while at the same time his invective, however exaggerated, seems to spring from real feelings; and what is pretence, and what sincerity, appears to me an insoluble problem. Something depends here on the further question whether or not Hamlet suspects or detects the presence of listeners; but, in the absence of an authentic stage tradition, this question too seems to be unanswerable.

But something further seems to follow from the considerations adduced. Hamlet's love, they seem to show, was not only mingled with bitterness, it was also, like all his healthy feelings, weakened and deadened by his melancholy. It was far from being extinguished; probably it was *one* of the causes which drove him to force his way to Ophelia; whenever he saw Ophelia, it awoke and, the circumstances being what they were, tormented him. But it was not an absorbing passion; it did not habitually occupy his thoughts; and when he declared that it was such a love as forty thousand brothers could not equal, he spoke sincerely indeed but not truly. What he said was true, if I may put it thus, of the inner healthy self which doubtless in time would have fully reasserted itself; but it was only partly true of the Hamlet whom we see in the play. And the morbid influence of his melancholy on his love is the cause of those strange facts, that he never alludes to her in his soliloquies, and that he appears not to realize how the death of her father must affect her.

The facts seem almost to force this idea on us. That it is less 'romantic' than the popular view is no argument against it. And psychologically it is quite sound, for a frequent symptom of such melancholy as Hamlet's is a more or less complete paralysis, or even perversion, of the emotion of love. And yet, while feeling no doubt that up to a certain point it is true, I confess I am not satisfied that the explanation of Hamlet's silence regarding Ophelia lies in it. (pp. 112–16) □

Bradley interrupted his progress through the play's action to consider some of the play's characters because that was how he encountered the play in imagination. Claudius comes last and the way Shakespeare has presented him leads to Bradley's most comprehensive view of the tragedy's action and his closest definition of its mysterious effect on an audience. This definition of Shakespeare's 'tragic vision' has arisen directly from the critic's close and questioning encounter with a playtext and his concern with the progressive experience of an audience or of a reader conscious of what may happen in performance.

■ King Claudius rarely gets from the reader the attention he deserves. But he is very interesting, both psychologically and dramatically. On the one hand, he is not without respectable qualities. As a king he is courteous and never undignified; he performs his ceremonial duties efficiently; and he takes good care of the national interests. He nowhere shows cowardice, and when Laertes and the mob force their way into the palace, he confronts a dangerous situation with coolness and address. His love for his ill-gotten wife seems to be quite genuine, and there is no ground for suspecting him of having used her as a mere means to the crown. His conscience, though ineffective, is far from being dead. In spite of its reproaches he plots new crimes to ensure the prize of the old one; but still it makes him unhappy (III.i.49f., III.iii.35f.). Nor is he cruel or malevolent.

On the other hand, he is no tragic character. He had a small nature. If Hamlet may be trusted, he was a man of mean appearance – a mildewed ear, a toad, a bat; and he was also bloated by excess in drinking. People made mouths at him in contempt while his brother lived; and though, when he came to the throne, they spent large sums in buying his portrait, he evidently put little reliance on their loyalty. He was no villain of force, who thought of winning his brother's crown by a bold and open stroke, but a cut purse who stole the diadem from a shelf and put it in his pocket. He had the inclination of natures physically weak and morally small towards intrigue and crooked dealing. His instinctive predilection was for poison: this was the means he used in his first murder, and he at once recurred to it when he had failed to get Hamlet executed by deputy. Though in danger he showed no cowardice, his first thought was always for himself.

> I like him not, nor stands it safe with *us*
> To let his madness range,

– these are the first words we hear him speak after the play-scene. His first comment on the death of Polonius is,

> It had been so with *us* had we been there;

and his second is,

> Alas, how shall this bloody deed be answered?
> It will be laid to *us*.

He was not, however, stupid, but rather quick-witted and adroit. He won the Queen partly indeed by presents (how pitifully characteristic of her!), but also by 'witch-craft of his wit' or intellect. He seems to have been soft-spoken, ingratiating in manner, and given to smiling on the person he addressed ('that one may smile, and smile, and be a villain'). We see this in his speech to Laertes about the young man's desire to return to Paris (I.ii.42f.). Hamlet scarcely ever speaks to him without an insult, but he never shows resentment, hardly even annoyance. He makes use of Laertes with great dexterity. He had evidently found that a clear head, a general complaisance, a willingness to bend and oblige where he could not overawe, would lead him to his objects – that he could trick men and manage them. Unfortunately he imagined he could trick something more than men.

This error, together with a decided trait of temperament, leads him to his ruin. He has a sanguine disposition. When first we see him, all has fallen out to his wishes, and he confidently looks forward to a happy life. He believes his secret to be absolutely safe, and he is quite ready to be kind to Hamlet, in whose melancholy he sees only excess of grief. He has no desire to see him leave the court; he promises him his voice for the succession (I.ii.108, III.ii.355); he will be a father to him. Before long, indeed, he becomes very uneasy, and then more and more alarmed; but when, much later, he has contrived Hamlet's death in England, he has still no suspicion that he need not hope for happiness:

> till I know 'tis done,
> Howe'er my haps, my *joys* were ne'er begun.

Nay, his very last words show that he goes to death unchanged:

> Oh yet defend me, friends, I am but hurt [= wounded],

he cries, although in half a minute he is dead. That his crime has failed, and that it could do nothing else, never once comes home to him. He thinks he can over-reach Heaven. When he is praying for pardon, he is all the while perfectly determined to keep his crown; and he knows it. More – it is one of the grimmest things in Shakespeare, but he puts such things so quietly that we are apt to miss them – when the King is praying for pardon for his first murder he has just made his final arrangements for a second, the murder of Hamlet. But he does not allude to that fact in his prayer. If Hamlet had really wished to kill him at a moment that had no relish of salvation in it, he had no need to wait. So we are inclined to say; and yet it was not so. For this was the crisis for Claudius as well as Hamlet. He had better have died at once, before he had added to his guilt a share in the responsibility for all the woe and death that followed. And so, we may allow ourselves to say, here also Hamlet's indiscretion served him well. The power that shaped his end shaped the King's no less.

For – to return in conclusion to the action of the play – in all that happens or is done we seem to apprehend some vaster power. We do not define it, or even name it, or perhaps even say to ourselves that it is there; but our imagination is haunted by the sense of it, as it works its way through the deeds or the delays of men to its inevitable end. And most of all do we feel this in regard to Hamlet and the King. For these two, the one by his shrinking from his appointed task, and the other by efforts growing ever more feverish to rid himself of his enemy, seem to be bent on avoiding each other. But they cannot. Through devious paths, the very paths they take in order to escape, something is pushing them silently step by step towards one another, until they meet and it puts the sword into Hamlet's hand. He himself must die, for he needed this compulsion before he could fulfil the demand of destiny; but he *must* fulfil it. And the King too, turn and twist as he may, must reach the appointed goal, and is only hastening to it by the windings which seem to lead elsewhere. Concentration on the character of the hero is apt to withdraw our attention from this aspect of the drama; but in no other tragedy of Shakespeare's, not even in *Macbeth*, is this aspect so impressive.

I mention *Macbeth* for a further reason. In *Macbeth* and *Hamlet* not only is the feeling of a supreme power or destiny peculiarly marked, but it has also at times a peculiar tone, which may be called, in a sense, religious. I cannot make my meaning clear without using language too definite to describe truly the imaginative impression produced; but it is roughly true that, while we do not imagine the supreme power as a divine being who avenges crime, or as a providence which supernaturally interferes, our sense of it is influenced by the fact that Shakespeare uses current religious ideas here much more decidedly than in *Othello* or *King Lear*. The horror in Macbeth's soul is more than once represented as desperation at the thought that he is eternally 'lost'; the same idea appears in the attempt of Claudius at repentance; and as *Hamlet* nears its close the 'religious' tone of the tragedy is deepened in two ways. In the first place, 'accident' is introduced into the plot in its barest and least dramatic form, when Hamlet is brought back to Denmark by the chance of the meeting with the pirate ship. This incident has been therefore severely criticized as a lame expedient, but it appears probable that the 'accident' is meant to impress the imagination as the very reverse of accidental, and with many readers it certainly does so. And that this was the intention is made the more likely by a second fact, the fact that in connection with the events of the voyage Shakespeare introduces that feeling, on Hamlet's part, of his being in the hands of Providence. The repeated expressions of this feeling are not, I have maintained, a sign that Hamlet has now formed a fixed resolution to do his duty forthwith; but their effect is to strengthen in the spectator the feeling that, whatever may become of Hamlet, and whether he wills it or not, his task will surely be accomplished, because it is the purpose of a power against which both he and his enemy are impotent, and which makes of them the instruments of its own will.

Observing this, we may remember another significant point of resemblance between *Hamlet* and *Macbeth*, the appearance in each play of a Ghost – a figure which seems quite in place in either, whereas it would seem utterly out of place in *Othello* or *King Lear*. Much might be said of the Ghost in *Hamlet*, but I confine myself to the matter which we are now considering. What is the effect of the appearance of the Ghost? And, in particular, why does Shakespeare make this Ghost so *majestical* a phantom, giving it that measured and solemn utterance, and that air of impersonal abstraction which forbids, for example, all expression of affection for Hamlet and checks in Hamlet the outburst of pity for his father? Whatever the intention may have been, the result is that the Ghost affects imagination not simply as the apparition of a dead king who desires the accomplishment of *his* purposes, but also as the representative of that hidden ultimate power, the messenger of divine justice set upon the expiation of offences which it appeared impossible for man to discover and avenge, a reminder of a symbol of the connection of the limited world of ordinary experience with the vaster life of which it is but a partial appearance. And as, at the beginning of the play, we have this intimation, conveyed through the medium of the received religious idea of a soul come from purgatory, so at the end, conveyed through the similar idea of a soul carried by angels to its rest, we have an intimation of the same character, and a reminder that the apparent failure of Hamlet's life is not the ultimate truth concerning him.

If these various peculiarities of the tragedy are considered, it will be agreed that, while *Hamlet* certainly cannot be called in the specific sense a 'religious drama', there is in it nevertheless both a freer use of popular religious ideas, and a more decided, though always imaginative, intimation of a supreme power concerned in human evil and good, than can be found in any other of Shakespeare's tragedies. And this is probably one of the causes of the special popularity of this play, just as *Macbeth*, the tragedy which in these respects most nearly approaches it, has also the place next to it in general esteem.   (pp. 124–9) □

CHAPTER NINE

Othello

■ There is practically no doubt that *Othello* was the tragedy written next after *Hamlet*. . . . But in point of substance, and, in certain respects, in point of style, the unlikeness of *Othello* to *Hamlet* is much greater than the likeness, and the later play belongs decidedly to one group with its successors. . . . Like them, it is a tragedy of passion, a description inapplicable to *Julius Caesar* or *Hamlet*. And with this change goes another, an enlargement in the stature of the hero. There is in most of the later heroes something colossal, something which reminds us of Michael Angelo's figures. They are not merely exceptional men, they are huge men; as it were, survivors of the heroic age living in a later and smaller world. We do not receive this impression from Romeo or Brutus or Hamlet, nor did it lie in Shakespeare's design to allow more than touches of this trait to Julius Caesar himself; but it is strongly marked in Lear and Coriolanus, and quite distinct in Macbeth and even in Antony. Othello is the first of these men, a being essentially large and grand, towering above his fellows, holding a volume of force which in repose ensures pre-eminence without an effort, and in commotion reminds us rather of the fury of the elements than of the tumult of common human passion.

★ ★ ★

What is the peculiarity of *Othello*? What is the distinctive impression that it leaves? Of all Shakespeare's tragedies, I would answer, not even excepting *King Lear*, *Othello* is the most painfully exciting and the most terrible. From the moment when the temptation of the hero begins, the reader's heart and mind are held in a vice, experiencing the extremes of pity and fear, sympathy and repulsion, sickening hope and dreadful expectation. Evil is displayed before him, not indeed with the profusion found in *King Lear*, but forming, as it were, the soul of a single character, and united with an intellectual superiority so great that he watches its advance fascinated and appalled. He sees it, in itself almost irresistible, aided at every step by fortunate accidents and the innocent mistakes of its victims. He seems to breathe an atmosphere as fateful as that of *King Lear*, but more confined and oppressive, the darkness not of night but of a close-shut murderous room. His imagination is excited to intense activity, but it is the activity of concentration rather than dilation. . . . But if we glance at some of its other sources, we shall find at the same time certain distinguishing characteristics of *Othello*. . . .

Othello is not only the most masterly of the tragedies in point of construction, but its method of construction is unusual. And this method, by which the conflict begins late, and advances without appreciable pause and with accelerating speed to the catastrophe, is a main cause of the painful tension just described. To this may be added that, after the conflict has begun, there is very little relief by way of the ridiculous. Henceforward at any rate Iago's humour never raises a smile. The clown is a poor one; we hardly attend to him and quickly forget him; I believe most readers of Shakespeare, if asked whether there is a clown in *Othello*, would answer No.

In the second place, there is no subject more exciting than sexual jealousy rising to the pitch of passion; and there can hardly be any spectacle at once so engrossing and so painful as that of a great nature suffering the torment of this passion, and driven by it to a crime which is also a hideous blunder. Such a passion as ambition, however terrible its results, is not itself ignoble; if we separate it in thought from the conditions which make it guilty, it does not appear despicable; it is not a kind of suffering, its nature is active; and therefore we can watch its course without shrinking. But jealousy, and especially sexual jealousy, brings with it a sense of shame and humiliation. For this reason it is generally hidden; if we perceive it we ourselves are ashamed and turn our eyes away; and when it is not hidden it commonly stirs contempt as well as pity. Nor is this all. Such jealousy as Othello's converts human nature into chaos, and liberates the beast in man; and it does this in relation to one of the most intense and also the most ideal of human feelings. What spectacle can be more painful than that of this feeling turned into a tortured mixture of longing and loathing, the 'golden purity' of passion split by poison into fragments, the animal in man forcing itself into his consciousness in naked grossness, and he writhing before it but powerless to deny it entrance, gasping inarticulate images of pollution, and finding relief only in a bestial thirst for blood? This is what we have to witness in one who was indeed 'great of heart' and no less pure and tender than he was great. . . .

The suffering of Desdemona ... [is] the most nearly intolerable spectacle that Shakespeare offers us. For one thing, it is *mere* suffering; and ... that is much worse to witness than suffering that issues in action. Desdemona is helplessly passive. She can do nothing whatever. She cannot retaliate even in speech; no, not even in silent feeling. And the chief reason of her helplessness only makes the sight of her suffering more exquisitely painful. She is helpless because her nature is infinitely sweet and her love absolute. ...

Turning from the hero and heroine to the third principal character, we observe (what has often been pointed out) that the action and catastrophe of *Othello* depend largely on intrigue. We must not say more than this. We must not call the play a tragedy of intrigue as distinguished from a tragedy of character. Iago's plot is Iago's character in action; and it is built on his knowledge of Othello's character, and could not otherwise have succeeded. Still it remains true that an elaborate plot was necessary to elicit the catastrophe; for Othello was no Leontes, and his was the last nature to engender such jealousy from itself. Accordingly Iago's intrigue occupies a position in the drama for which no parallel can be found in the other tragedies; the only approach, and that a distant one, being the intrigue of Edmund in the secondary plot of *King Lear*. Now in any novel or play, even if the persons rouse little interest and are never in serious danger, a skilfully-worked intrigue will excite eager attention and suspense. And where, as in *Othello*, the persons inspire the keenest sympathy and antipathy, and life and death depend on the intrigue, it becomes the source of a tension in which pain almost overpowers pleasure. Nowhere else in Shakespeare do we hold our breath in such anxiety and for so long a time as in the later Acts of *Othello*.

One result of the prominence of the element of intrigue is that *Othello* is less unlike a story of private life than any other of the great tragedies. And this impression is strengthened in further ways. In the other great tragedies the action is placed in a distant period, so that its general significance is perceived through a thin veil which separates the persons from ourselves and our own world. But *Othello* is a drama of modern life; when it first appeared it was a drama almost of contemporary life, for the date of the Turkish attack on Cyprus is 1570. The characters come close to us, and the application of the drama to ourselves (if the phrase may be pardoned) is more immediate than it can be in *Hamlet* or *Lear*. Besides this, their fortunes affect us as those of private individuals more than is possible in any of the later tragedies with the exception of *Timon*. I have not forgotten the Senate, nor Othello's position, nor his service to the State; but his deed and his death have not that influence on the interests of a nation or an empire which serves to idealize, and to remove far from our own sphere, the stories of Hamlet and Macbeth, of Coriolanus and Antony. Indeed he is already superseded at Cyprus when his fate is consummated, and as we leave him no vision rises on us, as in other tragedies, of peace descending on a distracted land.

The peculiarities so far considered combine with others to produce those feelings of oppression, of confinement to a comparatively narrow world, and of dark fatality, which haunt us in reading *Othello*. In *Macbeth* the fate which works itself out alike in the external conflict and in the hero's soul, is obviously hostile to evil; and the imagination is dilated both by the consciousness of its presence and by the appearance of supernatural agencies. These, as we have seen, produce in *Hamlet* a somewhat similar effect, which is increased by the hero's acceptance of the accidents as a providential shaping of his end. *King Lear* is undoubtedly the tragedy which comes nearest to *Othello* in the impression of darkness and fatefulness, and in the absence of direct indications of any guiding power. But in *King Lear*, apart from other differences to be considered later, the conflict assumes proportions so vast that the imagination seems, as in *Paradise Lost*, to traverse spaces wider than the earth. In reading *Othello* the mind is not thus distended. It is more bound down to the spectacle of noble beings caught in toils from which there is no escape; while the prominence of the intrigue diminishes the sense of the dependence of the catastrophe on character, and the part played by accident in this catastrophe accentuates the feeling of fate. This influence of accident is keenly felt in *King Lear* only once, and at the very end of the play. In *Othello*, after the temptation has begun, it is incessant and terrible. The skill of Iago was extraordinary, but so was his good fortune. Again and again a chance word from Desdemona, a chance meeting of Othello and Cassio, a question which starts to our lips and which anyone but Othello would have asked, would have destroyed Iago's plot and ended his life. In their stead, Desdemona drops her handkerchief at the moment most favourable to him, Cassio blunders into the presence of Othello only to find him in a swoon, Bianca arrives precisely when she is wanted to complete Othello's deception and incense his anger into fury. All this and much more seems to us quite natural, so potent is the art of the dramatist; but it confounds us with a feeling, such as we experience in the *Oedipus Tyrannus*, that for these star-crossed mortals . . . there is no escape from fate, and even with a feeling, absent from that play, that fate has taken sides with villainy. It is not surprising, therefore, that *Othello* should affect us as *Hamlet* and *Macbeth* never do, and as *King Lear* does only in slighter measure. On the contrary, it is marvellous that, before the tragedy is over, Shakespeare should have succeeded in toning down this impression into harmony with others more solemn and serene. (pp. 130–5) □

*After this introductory passage on the effect of the structural and narrative characteris-
tics of the tragedy, Bradley turns aside to deal with arguments against its success before
using a careful reading of the text to seek out the subtextual and instinctive characteristics of the principal persons in the play.*

■ The character of Othello is comparatively simple, but, as I have
dwelt on the prominence of intrigue and accident in the play, it is
desirable to show how essentially the success of Iago's plot is
connected with this character. Othello's description of himself as

> one not easily jealous, but, being wrought,
> Perplexed in the extreme,

is perfectly just. His tragedy lies in this – that his whole nature was indisposed to jealousy, and yet was such that he was unusually open to
deception, and, if once wrought to passion, likely to act with little reflection, with no delay, and in the most decisive manner conceivable. . . .

Othello is, in one sense of the word, by far the most romantic figure
among Shakespeare's heroes; and he is so partly from the strange life
of war and adventure which he has lived from childhood. He does not
belong to our world, and he seems to enter it we know not whence –
almost as if from wonderland. There is something mysterious in his
descent from men of royal siege; in his wanderings in vast deserts and
among marvellous peoples; in his tales of magic handkerchiefs and
prophetic Sibyls; in the sudden vague glimpses we get of numberless
battles and sieges in which he has played the hero and has borne a
charmed life; even in chance references to his baptism, his being sold
to slavery, his sojourn in Aleppo.

And he is not merely a romantic figure; his own nature is romantic. He has not indeed, the meditative or speculative imagination of
Hamlet; but in the strictest sense of the word he is more poetic than
Hamlet. Indeed, if one recalls Othello's most famous speeches –
those that begin, 'Her father loved me', 'O now for ever', 'Never,
Iago', 'Had it pleased Heaven', 'It is the cause', 'Behold, I have a
weapon', 'Soft you, a word or two before you go' – and if one places
side by side with these speeches an equal number by any other hero,
one will not doubt that Othello is the greatest poet of them all.
There is the same poetry in his casual phrases – like 'These nine
moons wasted', 'Keep up your bright swords, for the dew will rust
them', 'You chaste stars', 'It is a sword of Spain, the ice-brook's
temper', 'It is the very error of the moon' – and in those brief expressions of intense feeling which ever since have been taken as the
absolute expression, like

> If it were now to die,
> 'Twere now to be most happy; for, I fear,
> My soul hath her content so absolute
> That not another comfort like to this
> Succeeds in unknown fate,

or

> If she be false, O then Heaven mocks itself,
> I'll not believe it;

or

> No, my heart is turned to stone; I strike it, and it hurts my hand,

or

> But yet the pity of it, Iago! O Iago, the pity of it, Iago!

or

> O thou weed,
> Who are so lovely fair and smell'st so sweet
> That the sense aches at thee, would thou hadst ne'er been born.

And this imagination, we feel, has accompanied his whole life. He has watched with a poet's eye the Arabian trees dropping their med'cinable gum, and the Indian throwing away his chance-found pearl; and has gazed in a fascinated dream at the Pontic sea rushing, never to return, to the Propontic and the Hellespont; and has felt as no other man ever felt (for he speaks of it as none other ever did) the poetry of the pride, pomp, and circumstance of glorious war.

So he comes before us, dark and grand, with a light upon him from the sun where he was born; but no longer young, and now grave, self-controlled, steeled by the experience of countless perils, hardships and vicissitudes, at once simple and stately in bearing and in speech, a great man naturally modest but fully conscious of his worth, proud of his services to the state, unawed by dignitaries and unelated by honours, secure, it would seem, against all dangers from without and all rebellion from within. And he comes to have his life crowned with the final glory of love, a love as strange, adventurous and romantic as any passage of his eventful history, filling his heart with tenderness and his imagination with ecstasy. For there is no love, not that of Romeo in his youth, more steeped in imagination than Othello's.

The sources of danger in this character are revealed but too clearly by the story. In the first place, Othello's mind, for all its poetry, is very simple. He is not observant. His nature tends outward. He is quite free from introspection, and is not given to reflection. Emotion excites his imagination, but it confuses and dulls his intellect. On this side he is the very opposite of Hamlet, with whom, however, he shares a great openness and trustfulness of nature. In addition, he has little experience of the corrupt products of civilized life, and is ignorant of European women.

In the second place, for all his dignity and massive calm (and he has greater dignity than any other of Shakespeare's men), he is by nature full of the most vehement passion. Shakespeare emphasizes his self-control, not only by the wonderful pictures of the First Act, but by references to the past. Lodovico, amazed at his violence, exclaims:

Is this the noble Moor whom our full Senate
Call all in all sufficient? Is this the nature
Whom passion could not shake? whose solid virtue
The shot of accident nor dart of chance
Could neither graze nor pierce?

Iago, who has here no motive for lying, asks:

Can he be angry? I have seen the cannon
When it hath blown his ranks into the air,
And, like the devil, from his very arm
Puffed his own brother – and can he be angry?

This, and other aspects of his character, are best exhibited by a single line – one of Shakespeare's miracles – the words by which Othello silences in a moment the night-brawl between his attendants and those of Brabantio:

Keep up your bright swords, for the dew will rust them.

And the same self-control is strikingly shown where Othello endeavours to elicit some explanation of the fight between Cassio and Montano. Here, however, there occur ominous words, which make us feel how necessary was this self-control, and make us admire it the more:

     Now, by heaven,
My blood begins my safer guides to rule,
And passion, having my best judgment collied,
Assays to lead the way.

We remember these words later, when the sun of reason is 'collied', blackened and blotted out in total eclipse.

Lastly, Othello's nature is all of one piece. His trust, where he trusts, is absolute. Hesitation is almost impossible to him. He is extremely self-reliant, and decides and acts instantaneously. If stirred to indignation, as 'in Aleppo once', he answers with one lightning stroke. Love, if he loves, must be to him the heaven where either he must live or bear no life. If such a passion as jealousy seizes him, it will swell into a well-nigh incontrollable flood. He will press for immediate conviction or immediate relief. Convinced, he will act with the authority of a judge and the swiftness of a man in mortal pain. Undeceived, he will do like execution on himself. . . .

The Othello of the Fourth Act is Othello in his fall. His fall is never complete, but he is much changed. Towards the close of the Temptation-scene he becomes at times most terrible, but his grandeur remains almost undiminished. Even in the following scene (III.iv.), where he goes to test Desdemona in the matter of the handkerchief, and receives a fatal confirmation of her guilt, our sympathy with him is hardly touched by any feeling of humiliation. But in the Fourth Act 'Chaos has come'. A slight interval of time may be admitted here. It is but slight; for it was necessary for Iago to hurry on, and terribly dangerous to leave a chance for a meeting of Cassio with Othello; and his insight into Othello's nature taught him that his plan was to deliver blow on blow, and never to allow his victim to recover from the confusion of the first shock. Still there is a slight interval; and when Othello reappears we see at a glance that he is a changed man. He is physically exhausted, and his mind is dazed. He sees everything blurred through a mist of blood and tears. He has actually forgotten the incident of the handkerchief, and has to be reminded of it. When Iago, perceiving that he can now risk almost any lie, tells him that Cassio has confessed his guilt, Othello, the hero who has seemed to us only second to Coriolanus in physical power, trembles all over; he mutters disjointed words; a blackness suddenly intervenes between his eyes and the world; he takes it for the shuddering testimony of nature to the horror he has just heard, and he falls senseless to the ground. When he recovers it is to watch Cassio, as he imagines, laughing over his shame. It is an imposition so gross, and should have been one so perilous, that Iago would never have ventured it before. But he is safe now. The sight only adds to the confusion of intellect the madness of rage; and a ravenous thirst for revenge, contending with motions of infinite longing and regret, conquers them. The delay till night-fall is torture to him. His self-control has wholly deserted him, and he strikes his wife in the presence of the Venetian envoy. He is so lost to all sense of reality that he never asks himself what will follow the deaths of Cassio and his wife. An ineradicable instinct of justice, rather than any last quiver of hope, leads him to question Emilia; but nothing could convince him now, and there follows the dreadful scene of accusation; and then, to allow us the relief of burning hatred and burning tears, the interview of Desdemona with Iago, and that last talk of hers with Emilia, and her last song.

But before the end there is again a change. The supposed death of Cassio (V.i.) satiates the thirst for vengeance. The Othello who enters the bed-chamber with the words,

> It is the cause, it is the cause, my soul,

is not the man of the Fourth Act. The deed he is bound to do is no murder, but a sacrifice. He is to save Desdemona from herself, not in hate but in honour; in honour, and also in love. His anger has passed; a boundless sorrow has taken its place; and

> this sorrow's heavenly:
> It strikes where it doth love.

Even when, at the sight of her apparent obduracy, and at the hearing of words which by a crowning fatality can only reconvince him of her guilt, these feelings give way to others, it is to righteous indignation they give way, not to rage; and, terribly painful as this scene is, there is almost nothing here to diminish the admiration and love which heighten pity. And pity itself vanishes, and love and admiration alone remain, in the majestic dignity and sovereign ascendancy of the close. (pp. 138–47) □

Bradley's treatment of Othello's race and colour contains too much misinformation to warrant reproducing here. The first lecture concludes with a comparatively short account of Desdemona. This also is dated, most obviously in the use of words like beauty *and* soul, *but Bradley's main concern here is to show how Shakespeare controlled the progressive experience of audiences and readers.*

■ There is perhaps a certain excuse for our failure to rise to Shakespeare's meaning, and to realize how extraordinary and splendid a thing it was in a gentle Venetian girl to love Othello, and to assail fortune with such a 'downright violence and storm' as is expected only in a hero. It is that when first we hear of her marriage we have not yet seen the Desdemona of the later Acts; and therefore we do not perceive how astonishing this love and boldness must have been in a maiden so quiet and submissive. And when we watch her in her suffering and death we are so penetrated by the sense of her heavenly sweetness and self-surrender that we almost forget that she had shown herself quite as exceptional in the active assertion of her own soul and will. She tends to become to us predominantly pathetic, . . . as innocent as Miranda and as loving as Viola, yet suffering more deeply than Cordelia or Imogen. And she seems to lack that independence and strength of spirit which Cordelia and Imogen possess, and which in a manner raises them above suffering. She appears passive and defence-less, and can oppose to wrong nothing but the infinite endurance and forgiveness of a love that knows not how to resist or resent. . . . If her part were acted by an artist equal to Salvini, and with a Salvini for Othello, I doubt if the spectacle of the last two Acts would not be pronounced intolerable.

Of course this later impression of Desdemona is perfectly right, but it must be carried back and united with the earlier before we can see what Shakespeare imagined. Evidently, we are to understand, inno-cence, gentleness, sweetness, lovingness were the salient and, in a sense, the principal traits in Desdemona's character. She was, as her father supposed her to be,

> a maiden never bold,
> Of spirit so still and quiet that her motion
> Blushed at herself.

But suddenly there appeared something quite different – something which could never have appeared, for example, in Ophelia – a love not only full of romance but showing a strange freedom and energy of spirit, and leading to a most unusual boldness of action; and this action was carried through with a confidence and decision worthy of Juliet or Cordelia. Desdemona does not shrink before the Senate; and her language to her father, though deeply respectful, is firm enough to stir in us some sympathy with the old man who could not survive his daughter's loss. This then, we must understand, was the emergence in Desdemona, as she passed from girlhood to womanhood, of an indi-viduality and strength which if she had lived would have been gradu-ally fused with her more obvious qualities and have issued in a thousand actions, sweet and good, but surprising to her conventional or timid neighbours. And, indeed, we have already a slight example in her overflowing kindness, her boldness and her ill-fated persistence in pleading Cassio's cause. But the full ripening of her lovely and noble nature was not to be. In her brief wedded life she appeared again chiefly as the sweet and submissive being of her girlhood; and the strength of her soul, first evoked by love, found scope to show itself only in a love which, when harshly repulsed, blamed only its own pain; when bruised, only gave forth a more exquisite fragrance; and when rewarded with death, summoned its last labouring breath to save its murderer. . . .

In Desdemona's incapacity to resist there is also, in addition to her perfect love, something which is very characteristic. She is, in a sense, a child of nature. . . . She seems to know evil only by name, and, her inclinations being good, she acts on inclination. This trait, with its results, may be seen if we compare her, at the crises of the story, with Cordelia. In Desdemona's place, Cordelia, however frightened at Othello's anger about the lost handkerchief, would not have denied its loss. Painful experience had produced in her a conscious principle of rectitude and a proud hatred of falseness, which would have made a lie, even one wholly innocent in spirit, impossible to her; and the clear sense of justice and right would have led her, instead, to require an explanation of Othello's agitation which would have broken Iago's plot to pieces. In the same way, at the final crisis, no instinctive terror of death would have compelled Cordelia suddenly to relinquish her demand for justice and to plead for life. But these moments are fatal to Desdemona, who acts precisely as if she were guilty; and they are fatal because they ask for something which, it seems to us, could hardly be united with the peculiar beauty of her nature.

This beauty is all her own. Something as beautiful may be found in Cordelia, but not the same beauty. Desdemona, confronted with Lear's foolish but pathetic demand for a profession of love, could have done, I think, what Cordelia could not do – could have refused to compete with her sisters, and yet have made her father feel that she loved him well. And I doubt if Cordelia, 'falsely murdered', would have been capable of those last words of Desdemona – her answer to Emilia's 'O, who hath done this deed?'

> Nobody: I myself. Farewell.
> Commend me to my kind lord. O, farewell!

Were we intended to remember, as we hear this last 'falsehood', that other falsehood, 'It is not lost', and to feel that, alike in the momentary child's fear and the deathless woman's love, Desdemona is herself and herself alone?   (pp. 151–4) □

The second Lecture on Othello *is almost wholly concerned with Iago: Bradley probes the text for subtextual motives and repeatedly calls on 'every day' experiences as evidence of the probable response of a reader or audience.*

■ Evil has nowhere else been portrayed with such mastery as in the character of Iago. Richard III, for example, beside being less subtly conceived, is a far greater figure and a less repellent. His physical deformity, separating him from other men, seems to offer some excuse for his egoism. In spite of his egoism, too, he appears to us more than a mere individual; he is the representative of his family, the Fury of the House of York. Nor is he so negative as Iago: he has strong passions, he has admirations, and his conscience disturbs him. There is the glory of power about him. Though an excellent actor, he prefers force to fraud, and in his world there is no general illusion as to his true nature. . . .

Of Shakespeare's characters Falstaff, Hamlet, Iago, and Cleopatra (I name them in the order of their births) are probably the most wonderful. Of these, again, Hamlet and Iago, whose births come nearest together, are perhaps the most subtle. And if Iago had been a person as attractive as Hamlet, as many thousands of pages might have been written about him, containing as much criticism good and bad. . . . I propose, therefore, to approach the subject directly, and, first, to consider how Iago appeared to those who knew him, and what inferences may be drawn from their illusions; and then to ask what, if we judge from the play, his character really was. . . . One must constantly remember not to believe a syllable that Iago utters on any subject, including himself, until one has tested his statement by comparing it with known facts and with other statements of his own or of other people, and by considering whether he had in the particular circumstances any reason for telling a lie or for telling the truth. . . .

So prodigious does his self-control appear that a reader might be excused for feeling a doubt of its possibility. But there are certain observations and further inferences which, apart from confidence in Shakespeare, would remove this doubt. It is to be observed, first, that Iago was able to find a certain relief from the discomfort of hypocrisy in those caustic or cynical speeches which, being misinterpreted, only heightened confidence in his honesty. They acted as a safety valve, very much as Hamlet's pretended insanity did. Next, I would infer from the entire success of his hypocrisy – what may also be inferred on other grounds, and is of great importance – that he was by no means a man of strong feelings and passions, like Richard, but decidedly cold by temperament. Even so, his self-control was wonderful, but there never was in him any violent storm to be controlled. Thirdly, I would suggest that Iago, though thoroughly selfish and unfeeling, was not by nature malignant, nor even morose, but that, on the contrary, he had a superficial good-nature, the kind of good-nature that wins popularity and is often taken as the sign, not of a good digestion, but of a good heart. And lastly, it may be inferred that, before the giant crime which we witness, Iago had never been detected in any serious offence and may even never have been guilty of one, but had pursued a selfish but outwardly decent life, enjoying the excitement of war and of casual pleasures, but never yet meeting with any sufficient temptation to risk his position and advancement by a dangerous crime. So that, in fact, the tragedy of *Othello* is in a sense his tragedy too. It shows us not a violent man, like Richard, who spends his life in murder, but a thoroughly bad, *cold* man, who is at last tempted to let loose the forces within him, and is at once destroyed. . . .

It is not merely that he never betrays his true nature; he seems to be master of *all* the motions that might affect his will. In the most dangerous moments of his plot, when the least slip or accident would be fatal, he never shows a trace of nervousness. When Othello takes him by the throat he merely shifts his part with his usual instantaneous adroitness. When he is attacked and wounded at the end he is perfectly unmoved: you cannot believe for a moment that the pain of torture will ever open Iago's lips. He is equally unassailable by the temptations of indolence or of sensuality. It is difficult to imagine him inactive; and though he has an obscene mind, and doubtless took his pleasures when and how he chose, he certainly took them by choice and not from weakness, and if pleasure interfered with his purposes the holiest of ascetics would not put it more resolutely by. 'What should I do?' Roderigo whimpers to him; 'I confess it is my shame to be so fond; but it is not in my virtue to amend it'. He answers: 'Virtue! a fig! 'tis in ourselves that we are thus and thus'. It all depends on our will. Love is 'merely a lust of the blood and a permission of the will. Come, be a man. . . . Ere I would say I would drown myself for the love of a guinea-hen, I would change my humanity with a baboon'. Forget for a moment that love is for Iago the appetite of a baboon; forget that he is as little assailable by pity as by fear or pleasure; and you will acknowledge that this lordship of the will, which is his practice as well as his doctrine, is great, almost sublime. Indeed, in intellect (always within certain limits) and in will (considered as a mere power, and without regard to its objects) Iago *is* great.

To what end does he use these great powers? His creed – for he is no sceptic, he has a definite creed – is that absolute egoism is the only rational and proper attitude, and that conscience or honour or any kind of regard for others is an absurdity. He does not deny that this absurdity exists. He does not suppose that most people secretly share his creed, while pretending to hold up and practise another. On the contrary, he regards most people as honest fools. He declares that he has never yet met a man who knew how to love himself; and his one expression of admiration in the play is for servants

Who trimmed in forms and visages of duty,
Keep yet their hearts attending on themselves.

'These fellows,' he says, 'have some soul.' He professes to stand, and he attempts to stand, wholly outside the world of morality.

The existence of Iago's creed and of his corresponding practice is evidently connected with a characteristic in which he surpasses nearly all the other inhabitants of Shakespeare's world. Whatever he may once have been, he appears, when we meet him, to be almost destitute of humanity, of sympathetic or social feeling. He shows no trace of affection, and in presence of the most terrible suffering he shows either pleasure or an indifference which, if not complete, is nearly so. . . . There is, for instance, not the least sign of his enjoying the distress of Desdemona. But his sympathetic feelings are so abnormally feeble and cold that, when his dislike is roused, or when an indifferent person comes in the way of his purpose, there is scarcely anything within him to prevent his applying the torture.

What is it that provokes his dislike or hostility? Here again we must look closely. Iago has been represented as an incarnation of envy, as a man who, being determined to get on in the world, regards everyone else with enmity as his rival. But this idea, though containing truth, seems much exaggerated. Certainly he is devoted to himself; but if he were an eagerly ambitious man, surely we should see much more positive signs of this ambition; and surely too, with his great powers, he would already have risen high, instead of being a mere ensign. . . . [What] is clear is that Iago is keenly sensitive to anything that touches his pride or self-esteem. It would be most unjust to call him vain, but he has a high opinion of himself and a great contempt for others. He is quite aware of his superiority to them in certain respects; and he either disbelieves in or despises the qualities in which they are superior to him. Whatever disturbs or wounds his sense of superiority irritates him at once; and in *that* sense he is highly competitive. This is why the appointment of Cassio provokes him. This is why Cassio's scientific attainments provoke him. This is the reason of his jealousy of Emilia. He does not care for his wife; but the fear of another man's getting the better of him, and exposing him to pity or derision as an unfortunate husband, is wormwood to him; and as he is sure that no woman is virtuous at heart, this fear is ever with him. For much the same reason he has a spite against goodness in men . . . partly because it annoys his intellect as a stupidity; partly (though he hardly knows this) because it weakens his satisfaction with himself, and disturbs his faith that egoism is the right and proper thing; partly because, the world being such a fool, goodness is popular and prospers. But he, a man ten times as able as Cassio or even Othello, does not greatly prosper. Somehow, for all the stupidity of these open and generous people, they get on better than the 'fellow of some soul'. And this, though he is not particularly eager to get on, wounds his pride. Goodness therefore annoys him. He is always ready to scoff at it, and would like to strike at it. In ordinary circumstances these feelings of irritation are not vivid in Iago – *no* feeling is so – but they are constantly present.

★   ★   ★

Our task of analysis is not finished; but we are now in a position to consider the rise of Iago's tragedy. Why did he act as we see him acting in the play? What is the answer to that appeal of Othello's:

> Will you, I pray, demand that demi-devil
> Why he hath thus ensnared my soul and body?

This question Why? is *the* question about Iago, just as the question Why did Hamlet delay? is *the* question about Hamlet. Iago refused to answer it; but I will venture to say that he *could* not have answered it, any more than Hamlet could tell why he delayed. But Shakespeare knew the answer, and if these characters are great creations and not blunders we ought to be able to find it too.

Is it possible to elicit it from Iago himself against his will? He makes various statements to Roderigo, and he has several soliloquies. From these sources, and especially from the latter, we should learn something. For with Shakespeare soliloquy generally gives information regarding the secret springs as well as the outward course of the plot; and, moreover, it is a curious point of technique with him that the soliloquies of his villains sometimes read almost like explanations offered to the audience. . . .

Is the account which Iago gives of the causes of his action the true account? The answer of the most popular view will be, 'Yes. Iago was, as he says, chiefly incited by two things, the desire of advancement, and a hatred of Othello due principally to the affair of the lieutenancy. These are perfectly intelligible causes; we have only to add to them unusual ability and cruelty, and all is explained. . . .

The difficulty about this popular view is, in the first place, that it attributes to Iago what cannot be found in the Iago of the play. Its Iago is impelled by *passions*, a passion of ambition and a passion of hatred; for no ambition or hatred short of passion could drive a man who is evidently so clear-sighted, and who must hitherto have been so prudent, into a plot so extremely hazardous. Why, then, in the Iago of the play do we find no sign of these passions or of anything approaching to them? Why, if Shakespeare meant that Iago was impelled by them, does he suppress the signs of them? Surely not from want of ability to display them. The poet who painted Macbeth and Shylock understood his business. Who ever doubted Macbeth's ambition or

Shylock's hate? And what resemblance is there between these passions and any feeling that we can trace in Iago? The resemblance between a volcano in eruption and a flameless fire of coke. ... Passion, in Shakespeare's plays, is perfectly easy to recognize. What vestige of it, of passion unsatisfied or of passion gratified, is visible in Iago? None: that is the very horror of him. He has *less* passion than an ordinary man, and yet he does these frightful things. The only ground for attributing to him, I do not say a passionate hatred, but anything deserving the name of hatred at all, is his own statement, 'I hate Othello'; and we know what his statements are worth.

But the popular view, besides attributing to Iago what he does not show, ignores what he does show. It selects from his own account of his motives one or two, and drops the rest; and so it makes everything natural. But it fails to perceive how unnatural, how strange and suspicious, his own account is. Certainly he assigns motives enough; the difficulty is that he assigns so many. A man moved by simple passions due to simple causes does not stand fingering his feelings, industriously enumerating their sources, and groping about for new ones. But this is what Iago does. And this is not all. These motives appear and disappear in the most extraordinary manner. Resentment at Cassio's appointment is expressed in the first conversation with Roderigo, and from that moment is never once mentioned again in the whole play. Hatred of Othello is expressed in the First Act alone. Desire to get Cassio's place scarcely appears after the first soliloquy, and when it is gratified Iago does not refer to it by a single word. The suspicion of Cassio's intrigue with Emilia emerges suddenly, as an after-thought, not in the first soliloquy but the second, and then disappears for ever. Iago's 'love' of Desdemona is alluded to in the second soliloquy; there is not the faintest trace of it in word or deed either before or after. The mention of jealousy of Othello is followed by declarations that Othello is infatuated about Desdemona and is of a constant nature, and during Othello's sufferings Iago never shows a sign of the idea that he is now paying his rival in his own coin. In the second soliloquy he declares that he quite believes Cassio to be in love with Desdemona: it is obvious that he believes no such thing, for he never alludes to the idea again, and within a few hours describes Cassio in soliloquy as an honest fool. This final reason for ill-will to Cassio never appears till the Fifth Act.

What is the meaning of all this? Unless Shakespeare was out of his mind, it must have a meaning. And certainly this meaning is not contained in any of the popular accounts of Iago.

Is it contained then in Coleridge's word 'motive-hunting'? Yes, 'motive-hunting' exactly answers to the impression that Iago's soliloquies produce. He is pondering his design, and unconsciously trying to justify it to himself. He speaks of one or two real feelings, such as resentment against Othello, and he mentions one or two real causes of these feelings. But these are not enough for him. Along with them, or alone, there come into his head, only to leave it again, ideas and suspicions, the creations of his own baseness or uneasiness, some old, some new, caressed for a moment to feed his purpose and give it a reasonable look, but never really believed in, and never the main forces which are determining his action. In fact, I would venture to describe Iago in these soliloquies as a man setting out on a project which strongly attracts his desire, but at the same time conscious of a resistance to the desire, and unconsciously trying to argue the resistance away by assigning reasons for the project. He is the counterpart of Hamlet, who tried to find reasons for his delay in pursuing a design which excites his aversion. And most of Iago's reasons for actions are no more the real ones than Hamlet's reasons for delay were the real ones. Each is moved by forces which he does not understand; and it is probably no accident that these two studies of states psychologically so similar were produced at about the same period.

What then were the real moving forces of Iago's action? . . . [D]esire of advancement and resentment about the lieutenancy, though factors and indispensable factors in the cause of Iago's action, are neither the principal nor the most characteristic factors. To find these, let us return to our half-completed analysis of the character. Let us remember especially the keen sense of superiority, the contempt of others, the sensitiveness to everything which wounds these feelings, the spite against goodness in men as a thing not only stupid but, both in its nature and by its success, contrary to Iago's nature and irritating to his pride. Let us remember in addition the annoyance of having always to play a part, the consciousness of exceptional but unused ingenuity and address, the enjoyment of action, and the absence of fear. . . .

The most delightful thing to such a man would be something that gave an extreme satisfaction to his sense of power and superiority; and if it involved, secondly, the triumphant exertion of his abilities, and, thirdly, the excitement of danger, his delight would be consummated. And the moment most dangerous to such a man would be one when his sense of superiority had met with an affront, so that its habitual cra[v]ing was reinforced by resentment, while at the same time he saw an opportunity of satisfying it by subjecting to his will the very persons who had affronted it. Now, this is the temptation that comes to Iago. Othello's eminence, Othello's goodness, and his own dependence on Othello, must have been a perpetual annoyance to him. At *any* time he would have enjoyed befooling and tormenting Othello. Under ordinary circumstances he was restrained, chiefly by self-interest, in some slight degree perhaps by the faintest pulsations of conscience or humanity. But disappointment at the loss of the lieutenancy supplied the touch of lively resentment that was required to overcome these obstacles; and the prospect of satisfying the sense of power by mastering Othello through an intricate and hazardous intrigue now became irresistible. Iago did not clearly understand what was moving his desire; though he tried to give himself reasons for his action, even those that had some reality made but a small part of the motive force; one may almost say they were no more than the turning of the handle which admits the driving power into the machine. Only once does he appear to see something of the truth. It is when he uses the phrase 'to *plume up my will* in double knavery'.

To 'plume up the will', to heighten the sense of power or superiority – this seems to be the unconscious motive of many acts of cruelty which evidently do not spring chiefly from ill-will, and which therefore puzzle and sometimes horrify us most. It is often this that makes a man bully the wife or children of whom he is fond. The boy who torments another boy, as we say, 'for no reason', or who without any hatred for frogs tortures a frog, is pleased with his victim's pain, not from any disinterested love of evil or pleasure in pain, but mainly because this pain is the unmistakable proof of his own power over his victim. So it is with Iago. His thwarted sense of superiority wants satisfaction. What fuller satisfaction could it find than the consciousness that he is the master of the General who has undervalued him and of the rival who has been preferred to him; that these worthy people, who are so successful and popular and stupid, are mere puppets in his hands, but living puppets, who at the motion of his finger must contort themselves in agony while all the time they believe that he is their one true friend and comforter? It must have been an ecstasy of bliss to him. And this, granted a most abnormal deadness of human feeling, is, however horrible, perfectly intelligible. There is no mystery in the psychology of Iago; the mystery lies in a further question, which the drama has not to answer, the question why such a being should exist.

Iago's longing to satisfy the sense of power is, I think, the strongest of the forces that drive him on. But there are two others to be noticed. One is the pleasure in an action very difficult and perilous and, therefore, intensely exciting. This action sets all his powers on the strain. He feels the delight of one who executes successfully a feat thoroughly congenial to his special aptitude, and only just within his compass; and, as he is fearless by nature, the fact that a single slip will cost him his life only increases his pleasure. His exhilaration breaks out in the ghastly words with which he greets the sunrise after the night of the drunken tumult which has led to Cassio's disgrace: 'By the mass, 'tis morning. Pleasure and action make the hours seem short'. Here, however, the joy in exciting action is quickened by other feelings. It appears more simply elsewhere in such a way as to suggest that nothing but such actions gave him happiness, and that his happiness was greater if the action was destructive as well as exciting. We find it, for instance, in his gleeful cry to Roderigo, who proposes to shout to Brabantio in order to wake him and tell him of his daughter's flight:

> Do, with like timorous [*terrifying*] accent and dire yell
> As when, by night and negligence, the fire
> Is spied in populous cities.

All through that scene; again, in the scene where Cassio is attacked and Roderigo murdered; everywhere where Iago is in physical action, we catch this sound of almost feverish enjoyment. His blood, usually so cold and slow, is racing through his veins.

But Iago, finally, is not simply a man of action; he is an artist. His action is a plot, the intricate plot of a drama, and in the conception and execution of it he experiences the tension and the joy of artistic creation. 'He is,' says Hazlitt, 'an amateur of tragedy in real life; and, instead of employing his invention on imaginary characters or long-forgotten incidents, he takes the bolder and more dangerous course of getting up his plot at home, casts the principal parts among his nearest friends and connections, and rehearses it in downright earnest, with steady nerves and unabated resolution.' . . . Those to whom this idea is unfamiliar, and who may suspect it at first sight of being fanciful . . . may observe, to take only one point, the curious analogy between the early stages of dramatic composition and those soliloquies in which Iago broods over his plot, drawing at first only an outline, puzzled how to fix more than the main idea, and gradually seeing it develop and clarify as he works upon it or lets it work. Here at any rate Shakespeare put a good deal of himself into Iago. But the tragedian in real life was not the equal of the tragic poet. His psychology, as we shall see, was at fault, at a critical point, as Shakespeare's never was. And so his catastrophe came out wrong, and his piece was ruined.

Such, then, seem to be the chief ingredients of the force which, liberated by his resentment at Cassio's promotion, drives Iago from inactivity into action, and sustains him through it. And, to pass to a new point, this force completely possesses him; it is his fate. It is like the passion with which a tragic hero wholly identifies himself, and which bears him on to his doom. It is true that, once embarked on this course, Iago *could* not turn back, even if this passion did abate; and it is also true that he is compelled, by his success in convincing Othello, to advance to conclusions of which at the outset he did not dream. He is thus caught in his own web, and could not liberate himself if he would. But, in fact, he never shows a trace of wishing to do so, not a trace of hesitation, of looking back, or of fear, any more than of remorse; there is no ebb in the tide. As the crisis approaches there passes through his mind a fleeting doubt whether the deaths of Cassio and Roderigo are indispensable; but that uncertainty, which does not concern the main issue, is dismissed, and he goes forward with undiminished zest. Not even in his sleep – as in Richard's before his final battle – does any rebellion of outraged conscience or pity, or any foreboding of despair, force itself into clear consciousness. His fate – which is himself – has completely mastered him: so that, in the later scenes, where the improbability of the entire success of a design built on so many different falsehoods forces itself on the reader, Iago appears for moments not as a consummate schemer, but as a man absolutely infatuated and delivered over to certain destruction. . . .

★   ★   ★

Iago is not merely negative or evil – far from it. Those very forces that moved him and made his fate – sense of power, delight in performing a difficult and dangerous action, delight in the exercise of artistic skill – are not at all evil things. We sympathize with one or other of them almost every day of our lives. And, accordingly, though in Iago they are combined with something detestable and so contribute to evil, our perception of them is accompanied with sympathy. In the same way, Iago's insight, dexterity, quickness, address, and the like, are in themselves admirable things; the perfect man would possess them. And certainly he would possess also Iago's courage and self-control, and, like Iago, would stand above the impulses of mere feeling, lord of his inner world. All this goes to evil ends in Iago . . . [and] might apparently co-exist with absolute egoism and total want of humanity. [But] it is not true that in Iago this egoism and this want are absolute, and that in this sense he is a thing of mere evil. They are frightful, but if they were absolute Iago would be a monster, not a man. The fact is, he *tries* to make them absolute and cannot succeed; and the traces of conscience, shame and humanity, though faint, are discernible. If his egoism were absolute he would be perfectly indifferent to the opinion of others; and he clearly is not so. His very irritation at goodness, again, is a sign that his faith in his creed is not entirely firm; and it is not entirely firm because he himself has a perception, however dim, of the goodness of goodness. What is the meaning of the last reason he gives himself for killing Cassio:

> He hath a daily beauty in his life
> That makes me ugly?

Does he mean that he is ugly to others? Then he is not an absolute egoist. Does he mean that he is ugly to himself? Then he makes an open confession of moral sense. And, once more, if he really possessed no moral sense, we should never have heard those soliloquies which so clearly betray his uneasiness and his unconscious desire to persuade himself that he has some excuse for the villainy he contemplates. These seem to be indubitable proofs that, against his will, Iago is a little better than his creed, and has failed to withdraw himself wholly from the human atmosphere about him. And to these proofs I would add, though with less confidence, two others. Iago's momentary doubt towards the end whether Roderigo and Cassio must be killed has always surprised me. As a mere matter of calculation it is perfectly obvious that they must; and I believe his hesitation is not merely intellectual, it is another symptom of the obscure working of conscience or humanity. Lastly, is it not significant that, when once his plot has begun to develop, Iago never seeks the presence of Desdemona; that he seems to leave her as quickly as he can (III.iv.138); and that, when he is fetched by Emilia to see her in her distress (IV.ii.110ff.), we fail to catch in his words any sign of the pleasure he shows in Othello's misery, and seem rather to perceive a certain discomfort, and, if one dare say it, a faint touch of shame or remorse? This interpretation of the passage, I admit, is not inevitable, but to my mind (quite apart from any theorizing about Iago) it seems the natural one. And if it is right, Iago's discomfort is easily understood; for Desdemona is the one person concerned against whom it is impossible for him even to imagine a ground of resentment, and so an excuse for cruelty. . . .

That [Iago] is supremely wicked nobody will doubt . . . but to say that his intellectual power is supreme is to make a great mistake. . . . Compare him with Hamlet, and you perceive how miserably close is his intellectual horizon; that such a thing as a thought beyond the reaches of his soul has never come near him; that he is prosaic through and through, deaf and blind to all but a tiny fragment of the meaning of things. . . . He was destroyed by the power that he attacked, the power of love; and he was destroyed by it because he could not understand it; and he could not understand it because it was not in him. . . . His plot is shattered by a blow from a quarter where he never dreamt of danger. He knows his wife, he thinks. She is not over-scrupulous, she will do anything to please him, and she has learnt obedience. But one thing in her he does not know – that she *loves* her mistress and would face a hundred deaths sooner than see her fair fame darkened. There is genuine astonishment in his outburst 'What! Are you mad?' as it dawns upon him that she means to speak the truth about the handkerchief. But he might well have applied to himself the words she flings at Othello,

O gull! O dolt!
As ignorant as dirt!

The foulness of his own soul made him so ignorant that he built into the marvellous structure of his plot a piece of crass stupidity. (pp. 155–77) □

Bradley spent most of both Lectures on Othello *on a penetrating analysis of its three principal characters. A brief admission of this emphasis alerts readers to his underlying commitment to a general concept of 'truth to nature' and an instructional purpose for theatre.*

■ The characters of Cassio and Emilia hardly require analysis, and I will touch on them only from a single point of view. In their combination of excellences and defects they are good examples of that truth to nature which in dramatic art is the one unfailing source of moral instruction.   (p. 177) □

CHAPTER TEN

King Lear

■ When I read *King Lear* two impressions are left on my mind: [it] seems to me Shakespeare's greatest achievement, but . . . *not* his best play. And I find that I tend to consider it from two rather different points of view. When I regard it strictly as a drama, it appears to me, though in certain parts overwhelming, decidedly inferior as a whole to *Hamlet*, *Othello* and *Macbeth*. When I am feeling that it is greater than any of these, and the fullest revelation of Shakespeare's power, I find I am not regarding it simply as a drama, but am grouping it in my mind with works like the *Prometheus Vinctus* and the *Divine Comedy*, and even with the greatest symphonies of Beethoven and the statues in the Medici Chapel. . . .

That which makes the *peculiar* greatness of King Lear – the immense scope of the work; the mass and variety of intense experience which it contains; the interpenetration of sublime imagination, piercing pathos, and humour almost as moving as the pathos; the vastness of the convulsion both of nature and of human passion; the vagueness of the scene where the action takes place, and of the movements of the figures which cross this scene; the strange atmosphere, cold and dark, which strikes on us as we enter this scene, enfolding these figures and magnifying their dim outlines like a winter mist; the half-realized suggestions of vast universal powers working in the world of individual fates and passions – all this interferes with dramatic clearness even when the play is read, and in the theatre not only refuses to reveal itself fully through the senses but seems to be almost in contradiction with their reports. This is not so with the other great tragedies. No doubt, as Lamb declared, theatrical representation gives only a part of what we imagine when we read them; but there is no *conflict* between the representation and the imagination, because these tragedies are, in essentials, perfectly dramatic. But *King Lear*, as a whole, is imperfectly dramatic, and there is something in its very essence which is at war

with the senses, and demands a purely imaginative realization. . . .
[A]ppeal is made not so much to dramatic perception as to a rarer and
more strictly poetic kind of imagination.   (pp. 182–5) □

*Having set out this opposition between a theatrical response and an intellectual,
Bradley spends most of the first Lecture on examining the 'faults' of the play in an
attempt to understand its 'greatness' and 'mystery'.*

■ We may begin . . . by referring to two passages which have often
been criticized with injustice. The first is that where the blinded
Gloster, believing that he is going to leap down Dover cliff, does in
fact fall flat on the ground at his feet, and then is persuaded that he
has leaped down Dover cliff but has been miraculously preserved.
Imagine this incident transferred to *Othello*, and you realize how
completely the two tragedies differ in dramatic atmosphere. In *Othello*
it would be a shocking or a ludicrous dissonance, but it is in harmony
with the spirit of *King Lear*. And not only is this so, but, contrary to
expectation, it is not, if properly acted, in the least absurd on the stage.
The imagination and the feelings have been worked upon with such
effect by the description of the cliff, and by the portrayal of the old
man's despair and his son's courageous and loving wisdom, that we are
unconscious of the grotesqueness of the incident for common sense.

The second passage is more important, for it deals with the origin
of the whole conflict. The oft-repeated judgment that the first scene
of *King Lear* is absurdly improbable, and that no sane man would think
of dividing his kingdom among his daughters in proportion to the
strength of their several protestations of love, is much too harsh and is
based upon a strange misunderstanding. This scene acts effectively, and
to imagination the story is not at all incredible. It is merely strange,
like so many of the stories on which our romantic dramas are based.
Shakespeare, besides, has done a good deal to soften the improbability
of the legend, and he has done much more than the casual reader
perceives. The very first words of the drama, as Coleridge pointed out,
tell us that the division of the kingdom is already settled in all its
details, so that only the public announcement of it remains. Later we
find that the lines of division have already been drawn on the map of
Britain (l. 38), and again that Cordelia's share, which is her dowry, is
perfectly well known to Burgundy, if not to France (ll. 197, 245). That
then which is censured as absurd, the dependence of the division on
the speeches of the daughters, was in Lear's intention a mere form,
devised as a childish scheme to gratify his love of absolute power and
his hunger for assurances of devotion. And this scheme is perfectly in
character. We may even say that the main cause of its failure was not
that Goneril and Regan were exceptionally hypocritical, but that

Cordelia was exceptionally sincere and unbending. And it is essential to observe that its failure, and the consequent necessity of publicly reversing his whole well-known intention, is one source of Lear's extreme anger. He loved Cordelia most and knew that she loved him best, and the supreme moment to which he looked forward was that in which she should outdo her sisters in expressions of affection, and should be rewarded by that 'third' of the kingdom which was the most 'opulent'. And then – so it naturally seemed to him – she put him to open shame.

There is a further point, which seems to have escaped the attention of Coleridge and others. Part of the absurdity of Lear's plan is taken to be his idea of living with his three daughters in turn. But he never meant to do this. He meant to live with Cordelia, and with her alone. The scheme of his alternate monthly stay with Goneril and Regan is forced on him at the moment by what he thinks the undutifulness of his favourite child. In fact his whole original plan, though foolish and rash, was not a 'hideous rashness' or incredible folly. If carried out it would have had no such consequences as followed its alteration. It would probably have led quickly to war, but not to the agony which culminated in the storm upon the heath. The first scene, therefore, is not absurd, though it must be pronounced dramatically faulty in so far as it discloses the true position of affairs only to an attention more alert than can be expected in a theatrical audience or has been found in many critics of the play.

Let us turn next to two passages of another kind, the two which are mainly responsible for the accusation of excessive painfulness, and so for the distaste of many readers and the long theatrical eclipse of *King Lear*. The first of these is much the less important; it is the scene of the blinding of Gloster. The blinding of Gloster on the stage has been condemned almost universally; and surely with justice, because the mere physical horror of such a spectacle would in the theatre be a sensation so violent as to overpower the purely tragic emotions, and therefore the spectacle would seem revolting or shocking. But it is otherwise in reading. For mere imagination the physical horror, though not lost, is so far deadened that it can do its duty as a stimulus to pity, and to that appalled dismay at the extremity of human cruelty which it is of the essence of the tragedy to excite. Thus the blinding of Gloster belongs rightly to *King Lear* in its proper world of imagination; it is a blot upon *King Lear* as a stage-play.

But what are we to say of the second and far more important passage, the conclusion of the tragedy, the 'unhappy ending', as it is called, though the word 'unhappy' sounds almost ironical in its weakness? Is this too a blot upon *King Lear as* a stage-play? The question is not so easily answered as might appear. Doubtless we are right when we turn with disgust from Tate's sentimental alterations [in his stage adaptation of 1681], from his marriage of Edgar and Cordelia, and from that cheap moral which every one of Shakespeare's tragedies contradicts, 'that Truth and Virtue shall at last succeed'. But are we so sure that we are right when we unreservedly condemn the feeling which prompted these alterations, or at all events the feeling which beyond question comes naturally to many readers of *King Lear* who would like Tate as little as we? What they wish, though they have not always the courage to confess it even to themselves, is that the deaths of Edmund, Goneril, Regan and Gloster should be followed by the escape of Lear and Cordelia from death, and that we should be allowed to imagine the poor old King passing quietly in the home of his beloved child to the end which cannot be far off. Now, I do not dream of saying that we ought to wish this, so long as we regard *King Lear* simply as a work of poetic imagination. But if *King Lear* is to be considered strictly as a drama, or simply as we consider *Othello*, it is not so clear that the wish is unjustified. In fact I will take my courage in both hands and say boldly that I share it, and also that I believe Shakespeare would have ended his play thus had he taken the subject in hand a few years later, in the days of *Cymbeline* and the *Winter's Tale*. . . . This catastrophe, unlike those of all the other mature tragedies, does not seem at all inevitable. It is not even satisfactorily motived. In fact it seems expressly designed to fall suddenly like a bolt from a sky cleared by the vanished storm. . . .

A dramatic mistake in regard to the catastrophe, however, even supposing it to exist, would not seriously affect the whole play. The principal structural weakness of *King Lear* . . . arises chiefly from the double action, which is a peculiarity of *King Lear* among the tragedies. By the side of Lear, his daughters, Kent, and the Fool, who are the principal figures in the main plot, stand Gloster and his two sons, the chief persons of the secondary plot. . . . The number of essential characters is so large, their actions and movements are so complicated, and events towards the close crowd on one another so thickly, that the reader's attention, rapidly transferred from one centre of interest to another, is overstrained. He becomes, if not intellectually confused, at least emotionally fatigued. The battle, on which everything turns, scarcely affects him. The deaths of Edmund, Goneril, Regan and Gloster seem 'but trifles here'; and anything short of the incomparable pathos of the close would leave him cold. There is something almost ludicrous in the insignificance of this battle, when it is compared with the corresponding battles in *Julius Caesar* and *Macbeth*; and though there may have been further reasons for its insignificance, the main one is simply that there was no room to give it its due effect among such a host of competing interests. . . .

Added to these defects there are others, which suggest that in *King Lear* Shakespeare was less concerned than usual with dramatic fitness; improbabilities, inconsistencies, sayings and doings which suggest questions only to be answered by conjecture. The improbabilities in *King Lear* surely far surpass those of the other great tragedies in number and in grossness. And they are particularly noticeable in the secondary plot. For example, no sort of reason is given why Edgar, who lives in the same house with Edmund, should write a letter to him instead of speaking; and this is a letter absolutely damning to his character. Gloster was very foolish, but surely not so foolish as to pass unnoticed this improbability; or, if so foolish, what need for Edmund to forge a letter rather than a conversation, especially as Gloster appears to be unacquainted with his son's handwriting? Is it in character that Edgar should be persuaded without the slightest demur to avoid his father instead of confronting him and asking him the cause of his anger? Why in the world should Gloster, when expelled from his castle, wander painfully all the way to Dover simply in order to destroy himself (IV.i.80)? And is it not extraordinary that, after Gloster's attempted suicide, Edgar should first talk to him in the language of a gentleman, then to Oswald in his presence in broad peasant dialect, then again to Gloster in gentle language, and yet that Gloster should not manifest the least surprise?

Again, to take three instances of another kind: (*a*) only a fortnight seems to have elapsed between the first scene and the breach with Goneril; yet already there are rumours not only of war between Goneril and Regan but of the coming of a French army; and this, Kent says, is perhaps connected with the harshness of *both* the sisters to their father, although Regan has apparently had no opportunity of showing any harshness till the day before. (*b*) In the quarrel with Goneril Lear speaks of his having to dismiss fifty of his followers at a clap, yet she has neither mentioned any number nor had any opportunity of mentioning it off the stage. (*c*) Lear and Goneril, intending to hurry to Regan, both send off messengers to her, and both tell the messengers to bring back an answer. But it does not appear either how the messengers *could* return or what answer could be required, as their superiors are following them with the greatest speed.

Once more, (*a*) why does Edgar not reveal himself to his blind father, as he truly says he ought to have done? The answer is left to mere conjecture. (*b*) Why does Kent so carefully preserve his incognito till the last scene? He says he does it for an important purpose, but what the purpose is we have to guess. . . . No one of such defects is surprising when considered by itself, but their number is surely significant. Taken in conjunction with other symptoms it means that Shakespeare, set upon the dramatic effect of the great scenes and upon

certain effects not wholly dramatic, was exceptionally careless of prob-
ability, clearness and consistency in smaller matters, introducing what
was convenient or striking for a momentary purpose without troubling
himself about anything more than the moment. In presence of these
signs it seems doubtful whether his failure to give information about
the fate of the Fool was due to anything more than carelessness or an
impatient desire to reduce his overloaded material. . . .

★ ★ ★

How is it, now, that this defective drama so overpowers us that we are
either unconscious of its blemishes or regard them as almost irrelevant?
As soon as we turn to this question we recognize, not merely that *King
Lear* possesses purely dramatic qualities which far outweigh its defects,
but that its greatness consists partly in imaginative effects of a wider
kind. And, looking for the sources of these effects, we find among
them some of those very things which appeared to us dramatically
faulty or injurious. . . . That excess in the bulk of the material and the
number of figures, events and movements, while they interfere with
the clearness of vision, have at the same time a positive value for imagination. They give the feeling of vastness, the feeling not of a scene or
particular place, but of a world; or, to speak more accurately, of a
particular place which is also a world. This world is dim to us, partly
from its immensity, and partly because it is filled with gloom; and in
the gloom shapes approach and recede, whose half-seen faces and
motions touch us with dread, horror, or the most painful pity – sympathies and antipathies which we seem to be feeling not only for them
but for the whole race. This world, we are told, is called Britain; but
we should no more look for it in an atlas than for the place, called
Caucasus, where Prometheus was chained by Strength and Force and
comforted by the daughters of Ocean, or the place where [Dante's]
Farinata stands erect in his glowing tomb, '*Come avesse lo Inferno in gran
dispitto.*'

Consider next the double action. It has certain strictly dramatic
advantages, and may well have had its origin in purely dramatic
considerations. To go no further, the secondary plot fills out a story
which would by itself have been somewhat thin, and it provides a most
effective contrast between its personages and those of the main plot,
the tragic strength and stature of the latter being heightened by
comparison with the slighter build of the former. But its chief value
lies elsewhere, and is not merely dramatic. It lies in the fact – in
Shakespeare without a parallel – that the sub-plot simply repeats the
theme of the main story. Here, as there, we see an old man 'with a
white beard'. He, like Lear, is affectionate, unsuspicious, foolish, and

self-willed. He, too, wrongs deeply a child who loves him not less for the wrong. He, too, meets with monstrous ingratitude from the child whom he favours, and is tortured and driven to death. This repetition does not simply double the pain with which the tragedy is witnessed: it startles and terrifies by suggesting that the folly of Lear and the ingratitude of his daughters are no accidents or merely individual aberrations, but that in that dark cold world some fateful malignant influence is abroad, turning the hearts of the fathers against their children and of the children against their fathers, smiting the earth with a curse, so that the brother gives the brother to death and the father the son, blinding the eyes, maddening the brain, freezing the springs of pity, numbing all powers except the nerves of anguish and the dull lust of life.

Hence, too, as well as from other sources, comes that feeling which haunts us in *King Lear*, as though we were witnessing something universal – a conflict not so much of particular persons as of the powers of good and evil in the world. And the treatment of many of the characters confirms this feeling. Considered simply as psychological studies few of them, surely, are of the highest interest. Fine and subtle touches could not be absent from a work of Shakespeare's maturity; but, with the possible exception of Lear himself, no one of the characters strikes us as psychologically a *wonderful* creation, like Hamlet or Iago or even Macbeth; one or two seem even to be somewhat faint and thin. And, what is more significant, it is not quite natural to us to regard them from this point of view at all. Rather we observe a most unusual circumstance. If Lear, Gloster and Albany are set apart, the rest fall into two distinct groups, which are strongly, even violently, contrasted: Cordelia, Kent, Edgar, the Fool on one side, Goneril, Regan, Edmund, Cornwall, Oswald on the other. These characters are in various degrees individualized, most of them completely so; but still in each group there is a quality common to all the members, or one spirit breathing through them all. Here we have unselfish and devoted love, there hard self-seeking. On both sides, further, the common quality takes an extreme form; the love is incapable of being chilled by injury, the selfishness of being softened by pity; and, it may be added, this tendency to extremes is found again in the characters of Lear and Gloster, and is the main source of the accusations of improbability directed against their conduct at certain points. Hence the members of each group tend to appear, at least in part, as varieties of one species; the radical differences of the two species are emphasized in broad hard strokes; and the two are set in conflict, almost as if Shakespeare . . . were regarding Love and Hate as the two ultimate forces of the universe.

The presence in *King Lear* of so large a number of characters in whom love or self-seeking is so extreme, has another effect. They do not merely inspire in us emotions of unusual strength, but they also stir the intellect to wonder and speculation. How can there be such men and women? we ask ourselves. How comes it that humanity can take such absolutely opposite forms? And, in particular, to what omission of elements which should be present in human nature, or, if there is no omission, to what distortion of these elements is it due that such beings as some of these come to exist? This is a question which Iago (and perhaps no previous creation of Shakespeare's) forces us to ask, but in *King Lear* it is provoked again and again. And more, it seems to us that the author himself is asking this question. 'Then let them anatomize Regan, see what breeds about her heart. Is there any cause in nature that makes these hard hearts?' – the strain of thought which appears here seems to be present in some degree throughout the play. We seem to trace the tendency which, a few years later, produced Ariel and Caliban, the tendency of imagination to analyse and abstract, to decompose human nature into its constituent factors, and then to construct beings in whom one or more of these factors is absent or atrophied or only incipient. This, of course, is a tendency which produces symbols, allegories, personifications of qualities and abstract ideas; and we are accustomed to think it quite foreign to Shakespeare's genius, which was in the highest degree concrete. No doubt in the main we are right here; but it is hazardous to set limits to that genius. The Sonnets, if nothing else, may show us how easy it was to Shakespeare's mind to move in a world of 'Platonic' ideas; and, while it would be going too far to suggest that he was employing conscious symbolism or allegory in *King Lear*, it does appear to disclose a mode of imagination not so very far removed from the mode with which, we must remember, Shakespeare was perfectly familiar in Morality plays and in [Spenser's] *Fairy Queen*.

This same tendency shows itself in *King Lear* in other forms. To it is due the idea of monstrosity – of beings, actions, states of mind, which appear not only abnormal but absolutely contrary to nature; an idea, which, of course, is common enough in Shakespeare, but appears with unusual frequency in *King Lear*, for instance in the lines:

> Ingratitude, thou marble-hearted fiend,
> More hideous when thou show'st thee in a child
> Than the sea-monster!

or in the exclamation,

> Filial ingratitude!
> Is it not as this mouth should tear this hand
> For lifting food to't?

It appears in another shape in that most vivid passage where Albany, as he looks at the face which had bewitched him, now distorted with dreadful passions, suddenly sees it in a new light and exclaims in horror:

Thou changed and self-cover'd thing, for shame
Bemonster not thy feature. Were't my fitness
To let these hands obey my blood,
They are apt enough to dislocate and tear
Thy flesh and bones: howe'er thou art a fiend,
A woman's shape doth shield thee.

It appears once more in that exclamation of Kent's, as he listens to the description of Cordelia's grief:

It is the stars,
The stars above us, govern our conditions;
Else one self mate and mate could not beget
Such different issues.

(This is not the only sign that Shakespeare had been musing over heredity, and wondering how it comes about that the composition of two strains of blood or two parent souls can produce such astonishingly different products.)

This mode of thought is responsible, lastly, for a very striking characteristic of *King Lear* – one in which it has no parallel except *Timon* – the incessant references to the lower animals and man's likeness to them. These references are scattered broadcast through the whole play as though Shakespeare's mind were so busy with the subject that he could hardly write a page without some allusion to it. The dog, the horse, the cow, the sheep, the hog, the lion, the bear, the wolf, the fox, the monkey, the pole-cat, the civet-cat, the pelican, the owl, the crow, the chough, the wren, the fly, the butterfly, the rat, the mouse, the frog, the tadpole, the wall-newt, the water-newt, the worm – I am sure I cannot have completed the list, and some of them are mentioned again and again. Often, of course, and especially in the talk of Edgar as the Bedlam, they have no symbolical meaning; but not seldom, even in his talk, they are expressly referred to for their typical qualities – 'hog in sloth, fox in stealth, wolf in greediness, dog in madness, lion in prey', 'The fitchew nor the soiled horse goes to't With a more riotous appetite'. Sometimes a person in the drama is compared, openly or implicitly, with one of them. Goneril is a kite: her ingratitude has a serpent's tooth: she has struck her father most serpent-like upon the very heart: her visage is wolvish: she has tied sharp-toothed unkindness like a vulture on her father's breast: for her husband she is a gilded serpent: to Gloster her cruelty seems to have the fangs of a boar. She and Regan are dog-hearted: they are tigers, not daughters: each is an adder to the other: the flesh of each is covered with the fell of a beast. Oswald is a mongrel, and the son and heir of a mongrel: ducking to everyone in power, he is a wag-tail: white with fear, he is a goose. Gloster, for Regan, is an ingrateful fox: Albany, for his wife, has a cowish spirit and is milk-liver'd: when Edgar as the Bedlam first appeared to Lear he made him think a man a worm. As we read, the souls of all the beasts in turn seem to us to have entered the bodies of these mortals; horrible in their venom, savagery, lust, deceitfulness, sloth, cruelty, filthiness; miserable in their feebleness, nakedness, defencelessness, blindness; and man, 'consider him well', is even what they are. Shakespeare, to whom the idea of the transmigration of souls was familiar and had once been material for jest, seems to have been brooding on humanity in the light of it. It is remarkable, and some-what sad, that he seems to find none of man's better qualities in the world of the brutes (though he might well have found the prototype of the self-less love of Kent and Cordelia in the dog whom he so habit-ually maligns); but he seems to have been asking himself whether that which he loathes in man may not be due to some strange wrenching of this frame of things, through which the lower animal souls have found a lodgment in human forms, and there found – to the horror and confusion of the thinking mind – brains to forge, tongues to speak, and hands to act, enormities which no mere brute can conceive or execute. He shows us in *King Lear* these terrible forces bursting into monstrous life and flinging themselves upon those human beings who are weak and defenceless, partly from old age, but partly because they *are* human and lack the dreadful undivided energy of the beast. And the only comfort he might seem to hold out to us is the prospect that at least this bestial race, strong only where it is vile, cannot endure: though stars and gods are powerless, or careless, or empty dreams, yet there must be an end of this horrible world:

> It will come;
> Humanity must perforce prey on itself
> Like monsters of the deep. □

At this point, Bradley returns to his distinction between Shakespeare the dramatist who speaks to the senses and Shakespeare the poet who speaks to the imagination. Because he thought in terms of the theatre of his own day, which used 'elaborate scenery', he argues that, as a play, King Lear *is a flawed masterpiece; but the cumbersome realistic or melodramatic productions that Bradley knew are no longer to be seen. Today we may believe, as Shakespeare seems to have done, that theatre can speak simultaneously to both the senses and the imagination.*

■ The influence of all this on imagination as we read *King Lear* is very great; and it combines with other influences to convey to us, not in the form of distinct ideas but in the manner proper to poetry, the wider or universal significance of the spectacle presented to the inward eye. But the effect of theatrical exhibition is precisely the reverse. There the poetic atmosphere is dissipated; the meaning of the very words which create it passes half-realized; in obedience to the tyranny of the eye we conceive the characters as mere particular men and women; and all that mass of vague suggestion, if it enters the mind at all, appears in the shape of an allegory which we immediately reject. A similar conflict between imagination and sense will be found if we consider the dramatic centre of the whole tragedy, the Storm-scenes. The temptation of Othello and the scene of Duncan's murder may lose upon the stage, but they do not lose their essence, and they gain as well as lose. The Storm-scenes in *King Lear* gain nothing and their very essence is destroyed. . . . For imagination, that is to say, the explosions of Lear's passion, and the bursts of rain and thunder, are not, what for the senses they must be, two things, but manifestations of one thing. It is the powers of the tormented soul that we hear and see in the 'groans of roaring wind and rain' and the 'sheets of fire'; and they that, at intervals almost more overwhelming, sink back into darkness and silence. Nor yet is even this all; but, as those incessant references to wolf and tiger made us see humanity 'reeling back into the beast' and ravening against itself, so in the storm we seem to see Nature herself convulsed by the same horrible passions; the 'common mother',

Whose womb immeasureable and infinite breast
Teems and feeds all,

turning on her children, to complete the ruin they have wrought upon themselves. . . . Such poetry as cannot be transferred to the space behind the footlights, but has its being only in imagination. Here then is Shakespeare at his very greatest, but not the mere dramatist Shakespeare.

And now we may say this also of the catastrophe, which we found questionable from the strictly dramatic point of view. Its purpose is not merely dramatic. This sudden blow out of the darkness, which seems so far from inevitable, and which strikes down our reviving hopes for the victims of so much cruelty, seems now only what we might have expected in a world so wild and monstrous. It is as if Shakespeare said to us: 'Did you think weakness and innocence have any chance here? Were you beginning to dream that? I will show you it is not so.'

★　★　★

I come to a last point. As we contemplate this world, the question presses on us What can be the ultimate power that moves it, that excites this gigantic war and waste, or, perhaps, that suffers them and overrules them? And in *King Lear* this question is not left to us to ask, it is raised by the characters themselves. References to religious or irreligious beliefs and feelings are more frequent than is usual in Shakespeare's tragedies, as frequent perhaps as in his final plays. He introduces characteristic differences in the language of the different persons about fortune or the stars or the gods, and shows how the question What rules the world? is forced upon their minds. They answer it in their turn: Kent, for instance:

> It is the stars,
> The stars above us, govern our condition:

Edmund:

> Thou, nature, art my goddess; to thy law
> My services are bound:

and again,

> This is the excellent foppery of the world, that, when we are sick in fortune – often the surfeit of our own behaviour – we make guilty of our disasters the sun, the moon and the stars; as if we were villains by necessity, fools by heavenly compulsion, . . . and all that we are evil in by a divine thrusting on:

Gloster:

> As flies to wanton boys are we to the gods;
> They kill us for their sport;

Edgar:

> Think that the clearest gods, who make them honours
> Of men's impossibilities, have preserved thee.

Here we have four distinct theories of the nature of the ruling power. And besides this, in such of the characters as have any belief in gods who love good and hate evil, the spectacle of triumphant injustice or cruelty provokes questionings like those of Job, or else the thought, often repeated, of divine retribution. To Lear at one moment the storm seems the messenger of heaven:

> Let the great gods,
> That keep this dreadful pother o'er our heads,
> Find out their enemies now. Tremble, thou wretch,
> That hast within thee undivulged crimes. . . .

At another moment those habitual miseries of the poor, of which he has taken too little account, seem to him to accuse the gods of injustice:

> Take physic, pomp;
> Expose thyself to feel what wretches feel,
> That thou mayst shake the superflux to them
> And show the heavens more just;

and Gloster has almost the same thought (IV.i.67ff.). Gloster again, thinking of the cruelty of Lear's daughters, breaks out,

> but I shall see
> The winged vengeance overtake such children.

The servants who have witnessed the blinding of Gloster by Cornwall and Regan, cannot believe that cruelty so atrocious will pass unpunished. One cries,

> I'll never care what wickedness I do,
> If this man come to good;

and another,

> if she live long,
> And in the end meet the old course of death,
> Women will all turn monsters.

Albany greets the news of Cornwall's death with the exclamation,

> This shows you are above,
> You justicers, that these our nether crimes
> So speedily can venge;

and the news of the deaths of the sisters with the words,

> This judgment of the heavens, that makes us tremble,
> Touches us not with pity.

Edgar, speaking to Edmund of their father, declares

> The gods are just, and of our pleasant vices
> Make instruments to plague us,

and Edmund himself assents. Almost throughout the latter half of the drama we note in most of the better characters a preoccupation with the question of the ultimate power, and a passionate need to explain by reference to it what otherwise would drive them to despair. And the influence of this preoccupation and need joins with other influences in affecting the imagination, and in causing it to receive from *King Lear* an impression which is at least as near of kin to the *Divine Comedy* as to *Othello*.

For Dante that which is recorded in the *Divine Comedy* was the justice and love of God. What did *King Lear* record for Shakespeare? Something, it would seem, very different. This is certainly the most terrible picture that Shakespeare painted of the world. In no other of his tragedies does humanity appear more pitiably infirm or more hopelessly bad. . . . The repetition of the main theme in that of the underplot, the comparisons of man with the most wretched and the most horrible of the beasts, the impression of Nature's hostility to him, the irony of the unexpected catastrophe – these, with much else, seem even to indicate an intention to show things at their worst, and to return the sternest of replies to that question of the ultimate power and those appeals for retribution. Is it an accident, for example, that Lear's . . . appeal, heart-rending in its piteousness,

> You see me here, you gods, a poor old man,
> As full of grief as age; wretched in both:

is immediately answered from the heavens by the sound of the breaking storm. Albany and Edgar may moralize on the divine justice as they will, but how, in the face of all that we see, shall we believe that they speak Shakespeare's mind? Is not his mind rather expressed in the bitter contrast between their faith and the events we witness, or in the scornful rebuke of those who take upon them the mystery of things as if they were God's spies? Is it not Shakespeare's judgment on his kind that we hear in Lear's appeal:

> And thou, all-shaking thunder,
> Smite flat the thick rotundity o' the world!
> Crack nature's moulds, all germens spill at once,
> That make ingrateful man!

and Shakespeare's judgment on the worth of existence that we hear in Lear's agonized cry, 'No, no, no life!'?

Most of the remarks made on *King Lear* in the present lecture, emphasize only certain aspects of the play and certain elements in the total impression. . . . The effect of these aspects, though far from being lost, is modified by that of others. I do not mean . . . that *King Lear* contains a revelation of righteous omnipotence or heavenly harmony, or even a promise of the reconciliation of mystery and justice. But then, as we saw, neither do Shakespeare's other tragedies contain these things. . . . There never was vainer labour than that of critics who try to make out that the persons in these dramas meet with 'justice' or their 'deserts'. But, on the other hand, man is not represented in these tragedies as the mere plaything of a blind or capricious power, suffering woes which have no relation to his character and actions; nor is the world represented as given over to darkness. And in these respects *King Lear*, though the most terrible of these works, does not differ in essence from the rest. Its keynote is surely to be heard neither in the words wrung from Gloster in his anguish, nor in Edgar's words 'the gods are just'. Its final and total result is one in which pity and terror, carried perhaps to the extreme limits of art, are so blended with a sense of law and beauty that we feel at last, not depression and much less despair, but a consciousness of greatness in pain, and of solemnity in the mystery we cannot fathom.   (pp. 186–210) □

Finding what he called a 'mystery' at the heart of this tragedy, Bradley spent more words on King Lear *than on any other tragedy but, having considered the play's structure and the audience's experience of a performance, he could give its characters less attention than was his custom. In the first Lecture he views them in relation to the wider interests of the tragedy, in the second he analyses them as individuals.*

■ The position of the hero in this tragedy is in one important respect peculiar. . . . When the conclusion arrives, the old King has for a long while been passive. We have long regarded him not only as 'a man more sinned against than sinning', but almost wholly as a sufferer, hardly at all as an agent. . . . Yet it is essential that Lear's contribution to the action of the drama should be remembered; not at all in order that we may feel that he 'deserved' what he suffered, but because otherwise his fate would appear to us at best pathetic, at worst shocking, but certainly not tragic. And when we were reading the earlier scenes of the play we recognized this contribution clearly enough. . . . A long life of absolute power, in which he has been flattered to the top of his bent, has produced in him that blindness to human limitations, and that presumptuous self-will, which in Greek tragedy we have so often seen stumbling against the altar of Nemesis. . . . The *injustice* of his rejection of Cordelia is shown most strikingly in the first scene when *immediately* upon the apparently cold words of Cordelia, 'So young, my lord, and true', there comes this dreadful answer:

> Let it be so; thy truth then be thy dower.
> For, by the sacred radiance of the sun,
> The mysteries of Hecate and the night;
> By all the operation of the orbs
> From whom we do exist and cease to be;
> Here I disclaim all my paternal care,
> Propinquity and property of blood,
> And as a stranger to my heart and me
> Hold thee from this for ever. The barbarous Scythian,
> Or he that makes his generation messes
> To gorge his appetite, shall to my bosom
> Be as well neighbour'd, pitied and relieved,
> As thou my sometime daughter.

Now the dramatic effect of this passage is exactly, and doubtless intentionally, repeated in the curse pronounced against Goneril. This does not come after the daughters have openly and wholly turned against their father. Up to the moment of its utterance Goneril has done no more than to require him 'a little to disquantity' and reform his train of knights. Certainly her manner and spirit in making this demand are hateful, and probably her accusations against the knights are false; and we should expect from any father in Lear's position passionate distress and indignation. But surely the famous words which form Lear's immediate reply were meant to be nothing short of frightful:

> Hear, nature, hear; dear goddess, hear!
> Suspend thy purpose, if thou didst intend
> To make this creature fruitful!
> Into her womb convey sterility!
> Dry up in her the organs of increase;
> And from her derogate body never spring
> A babe to honour her! If she must teem,
> Create her child of spleen; that it may live,
> And be a thwart disnatured torment to her!
> Let it stamp wrinkles in her brow of youth;
> With cadent tears fret channels in her cheeks;
> Turn all her mother's pains and benefits
> To laughter and contempt; that she may feel
> How sharper than a serpent's tooth it is
> To have a thankless child!

The question is not whether Goneril deserves these appalling imprecations, but what they tell us about Lear. They show that, although he has already recognized his injustice towards Cordelia, is secretly blaming himself, and is endeavouring to do better, the disposition from which his first error sprang is still unchanged. And it is precisely the disposition to give rise, in evil surroundings, to calamities dreadful but at the same time tragic, because due in some measure to the person who endures them.

The perception of this connection, if it is not lost as the play advances, does not at all diminish our pity for Lear, but it makes it impossible for us permanently to regard the world displayed in this tragedy as subject to a mere arbitrary or malicious power. It makes us feel that this world is so far at least a rational and a moral order, that there holds in it the law, not of proportionate requital, but of strict connection between act and consequence. It is, so far, the world of all Shakespeare's tragedies.

But there is another aspect of Lear's story, the influence of which modifies, in a way quite different and more peculiar to this tragedy, the impressions called pessimistic and even this impression of law. There is nothing more noble and beautiful in literature than Shakespeare's exposition of the effect of suffering in reviving the greatness and eliciting the sweetness of Lear's nature. The occasional recurrence, during his madness, of autocratic impatience or of desire for revenge serves only to heighten this effect, and the moments when his insanity becomes merely infinitely piteous do not weaken it. The old King who in pleading with his daughters feels so intensely his own humiliation and their horrible ingratitude, and who yet, at fourscore and upward, constrains himself to practise a self-control and patience so many years disused; who out of old affection for his Fool, and in repentance for his injustice to the Fool's beloved mistress, tolerates incessant and cutting reminders of his own folly and wrong; ... who comes in his affliction to think of others first, and to seek, in tender solicitude for his poor boy, the shelter he scorns for his own bare head; who learns to feel and to pray for the miserable and houseless poor, to discern the falseness of flattery and the brutality of authority, and to pierce below the differences of rank and raiment to the common humanity beneath; whose sight is so purged by scalding tears that it sees at last how power and place and all things in the world are vanity except love; who tastes in his last hours the extremes both of love's rapture and of its agony, but could never, if he lived on or lived again, care a jot for aught beside – there is no figure, surely, in the world of poetry at once so grand, so pathetic, and so beautiful as his. Well, but Lear owes the whole of this to those sufferings which made us doubt whether life were not simply evil, and men like the flies which wanton boys torture for their sport. Should we not be at least as near the truth if we called this poem *The Redemption of King Lear*, and declared that the business of 'the gods' with him was neither to torment him, nor to teach him a 'noble anger', but to lead him to attain through apparently hopeless failure the very end and aim of life? One can believe that Shakespeare had been tempted at times to feel misanthropy and despair, but it is quite impossible that he can have been mastered by such feelings at the time when he produced this conception. . . .

Much has been written on the representation of insanity in *King Lear*, and I will confine myself to one or two points which may have escaped notice. The most obvious symptom of Lear's insanity, especially in its first stages, is of course the domination of a fixed idea. Whatever presents itself to his senses, is seized on by this idea and compelled to express it; as for example in those words . . . which first show that his mind has actually given way:

> Hast thou given all
> To thy two daughters? And art thou come to this?

But it is remarkable that what we have here is only, in an exaggerated and perverted form, the very same action of imagination that, just before the breakdown of reason, produced . . .

> O heavens,
> If you do love old men, if your sweet sway
> Allow obedience, if yourselves are old,
> Make it your cause;

and

> I tax not you, you elements, with unkindness;
> I never gave you kingdom, call'd you children,
> You owe me no subscription: then let fall
> Your horrible pleasure; here I stand, your slave,
> A poor, infirm, weak, and despised old man: . . .

Shakespeare, long before this, in the *Midsummer Night's Dream*, had noticed the resemblance between the lunatic, the lover, and the poet; and the partial truth that genius is allied to insanity was quite familiar to him. But he presents here the supplementary half-truth that insanity is allied to genius. . . .

Lear's insanity, which destroys the coherence, also reduces the poetry of his imagination. What it stimulates is that power of moral perception and reflection which had already been quickened by his sufferings. This, however partial and however disconnectedly used, first appears, quite soon after the insanity has declared itself, in the idea that the naked beggar represents truth and reality, in contrast with those conventions, flatteries, and corruptions of the great world, by which Lear has so long been deceived and will never be deceived again:

> Is man no more than this? Consider him well. Thou owest the worm no silk, the beast no hide, the sheep no wool, the cat no perfume. Ha! here's three on's are sophisticated: thou art the thing itself.

Lear regards the beggar therefore with reverence and delight, as a person who is in the secret of things, and he longs to question him about their causes. It is this same strain of thought which much later (IV.vi.), gaining far greater force, though the insanity has otherwise advanced, issues in those famous Timon-like speeches which make us realize the original strength of the old King's mind. And when this strain, on his recovery, unites with the streams of repentance and love, it produces that serene renunciation of the world, with its power and glory and resentments and revenges, which is expressed in the speech (V.iii.):

> No, no, no, no! Come, let's away to prison:
> We two alone will sing like birds i' the cage:
> When thou dost ask me blessing, I'll kneel down,
> And ask of thee forgiveness: so we'll live,
> And pray, and sing, and tell old tales, and laugh
> At gilded butterflies, and hear poor rogues
> Talk of court news; and we'll talk with them too:
> Who loses, and who wins; who's in, who's out;
> And take upon's the mystery of things,
> As if we were God's spies: and we'll wear out,
> In a wall'd prison, packs and sets of great ones,
> That ebb and flow by the moon.

This is that renunciation which is at the same time a sacrifice offered to the gods, and on which the gods themselves throw incense; and, it may be, it would never have been offered but for the knowledge that came to Lear in his madness.

I spoke of Lear's 'recovery', but the word is too strong. The Lear of the Fifth Act is not indeed insane, but his mind is greatly enfeebled. The speech just quoted is followed by a sudden flash of the old passionate nature, reminding us most pathetically of Lear's efforts, just before his madness, to restrain his tears:

> Wipe thine eyes:
> The good-years shall devour them, flesh and fell,
> Ere they shall make us weep: we'll see 'em starve first.

And this weakness is still more pathetically shown in the blindness of the old King to his position now that he and Cordelia are made prisoners. It is evident that Cordelia knows well what mercy her father is likely to receive from her sisters; that is the reason of her weeping. But he does not understand her tears; it never crosses his mind that they have anything more than imprisonment to fear. And what is that to them? They have made that sacrifice, and all is well:

> Have I caught thee?
> He that parts us shall bring a brand from heaven,
> And fire us hence like foxes.

This blindness is most affecting to us, who know in what manner *they* will be parted; but it is also comforting. And we find the same mingling of effects in the overwhelming conclusion of the story. If to the reader, as to the bystanders, that scene brings one unbroken pain, it is not so with Lear himself. His shattered mind passes from the first transports of hope and despair, as he bends over Cordelia's body and holds the feather to her lips, into an absolute forgetfulness of the cause of these transports. This continues so long as he can converse with Kent; becomes an almost complete vacancy; and is disturbed only to yield, as his eyes suddenly fall again on his child's corpse, to an agony which at once breaks his heart. And, finally, though he is killed by an agony of pain, the agony in which he actually dies is one not of pain but of ecstasy. Suddenly, with a cry represented in the oldest text by a four-times repeated 'O', he exclaims:

> Do you see this? Look on her, look, her lips,
> Look there, look there!

These are the last words of Lear. He is sure, at last, that she *lives*: and what had he said when he was still in doubt?

> She lives! if it be so,
> It is a chance which does redeem all sorrows
> That ever I have felt!

To us, perhaps, the knowledge that he is deceived may bring a culmination of pain: but, if it brings *only* that, I believe we are false to Shakespeare, and it seems almost beyond question that any actor is false to the text who does not attempt to express, in Lear's last accents and gestures and look, an unbearable *joy*.

To dwell on the pathos of Lear's last speech would be an impertinence, but I may add a remark on the speech from the literary point of view. In the simplicity of its language, which consists almost wholly of monosyllables of native origin, composed in very brief sentences of the plainest structure, it presents an extraordinary contrast to the dying speech of Hamlet and the last words of Othello to the bystanders. The fact that Lear speaks in passion is one cause of the difference, but not the sole cause. The language is more than simple, it is familiar. And this familiarity is characteristic of Lear (except at certain moments, already referred to) from the time of his madness onwards, and is the source of the peculiarly poignant effect of some of his sentences (such as 'The little dogs and all . . .'). We feel in them the loss of power to sustain his royal dignity; we feel also that everything external has become nothingness to him, and that what remains is 'the thing itself', the soul in its bare greatness. Hence also it is that two lines in this last speech show, better perhaps than another passage of poetry, one of the qualities we have in mind when we distinguish poetry as 'romantic'. Nothing like Hamlet's mysterious sigh 'The rest is silence', nothing like Othello's memories of his life of marvel and achievement, was possible to Lear. Those last thoughts are romantic in their strangeness: Lear's five-times repeated 'Never', in which the simplest and most unanswerable cry of anguish rises note by note till the heart breaks, is romantic in its naturalism; and to make a verse out of this one word required the boldness as well as the inspiration which came infallibly to Shakespeare at the greatest moments. But the familiarity, boldness and inspiration are surpassed (if that can be) by the next line, which shows the bodily oppression asking for bodily relief . . . '[Pray you,] undo this button.'   (pp. 211–22)   □

Other dramatis personæ *are dealt with more briefly, for the most part as two contrasting groups of individuals, rather than as members belonging to a common and changing society that is divided within itself.*

■ Gloster and Albany are the two neutral characters of the tragedy. The parallel between Lear and Gloster, already noticed, is, up to a certain point, so marked that it cannot possibly be accidental. Both are old white-haired men (III.vii.37); both, it would seem, widowers, with children comparatively young. Like Lear, Gloster is tormented, and his life is sought, by the child whom he favours; he is tended and healed by the child whom he has wronged. His sufferings, like Lear's, are partly traceable to his own extreme folly and injustice, and, it may be added, to a selfish pursuit of his own pleasure. His sufferings, again, like Lear's, purify and enlighten him: he dies a better and wiser man than he showed himself at first. . . . And, finally, Gloster dies almost as Lear dies. Edgar reveals himself to him and asks his blessing (as Cordelia asks Lear's)

> but his flaw'd heart –
> Alack, too weak the conflict to support –
> 'Twixt two extremes of passion, joy and grief,
> Burst smilingly.

[But Gloster . . .] has infinitely less force and fire [than his master].

The combination of parallelism and contrast that we observe in Lear and Gloster, and again in the attitude of the two brothers to their father's superstition, is one of many indications that in *King Lear* Shakespeare was working more than usual on a basis of conscious and reflective ideas. Perhaps it is not by accident, then, that he makes Edgar and Lear preach to Gloster in precisely the same strain. Lear says to him . . . 'Thou must be patient; we came crying hither' . . . Edgar's last words to him are: 'Men must endure / Their going hence, even as their coming hither . . .'.

[Albany also] ends a better and wiser man than he began. . . . He is an inoffensive peace-loving man, and is overborne at first by his 'great love' for his wife and by her imperious will. He is not free from responsibility for the treatment which the King receives in his house; the Knight says to Lear, 'there's a great abatement of kindness appears as well in the general dependants as in *the duke himself also* and your daughter'. But he takes no part in the quarrel, and doubtless speaks truly when he protests that he is as guiltless as ignorant of the cause of Lear's violent passion. When the King departs, he begins to remonstrate with Goneril, but shrinks in a cowardly manner, which is a trifle comical, from contest with her. She leaves him behind when she goes to join Regan, and he is not further responsible for what follows. When he hears of it, he is struck with horror: the scales drop from his eyes, Goneril becomes hateful to him, he determines to revenge Gloster's eyes. His position is however very difficult, as he is willing to fight against Cordelia in so far as her army is French, and unwilling in so far as she represents her father. . . . The battle is not won by him but by Edmund; and but for Edgar he would certainly have fallen a victim to the murderous plot against him. When it is discovered, however, he is fearless and resolute enough, besides being full of kind feeling towards Kent and Edgar, and of sympathetic distress at Gloster's death. . . .

I turn now to those two strongly contrasted groups of good and evil beings. . . . In its representation of evil *King Lear* differs from the other tragedies only in degree and manner. It is the tragedy in which evil is shown in the greatest abundance; and the evil characters are peculiarly repellent from their hard savagery, and because so little good is mingled with their evil. The effect is therefore more startling than elsewhere; it is even appalling. . . . We see a world which generates terrible evil in profusion. Further, the beings in whom this evil appears at its strongest are able, to a certain extent, to thrive. They are not unhappy, and they have power to spread misery and destruction around them. All this is undeniable fact. On the other hand this evil is *merely* destructive: it founds nothing, and seems capable of existing only on foundations laid by its opposite. It is also self-destructive: it sets those beings at enmity; they can scarcely unite against a common and pressing danger; if it were averted they would be at each other's throats in a moment; the sisters do not even wait till it is past. Finally, these beings, all five of them, are dead a few weeks after we see them first; three at least die young; the outburst of their evil is fatal to them. . . .

The world in which evil appears . . . reacts against it violently, and, in the struggle to expel it, is driven to devastate itself. If we ask why the world should generate that which convulses and wastes it, the tragedy gives no answer, and we are trying to go beyond tragedy in seeking one. But the world, in this tragic picture, is convulsed by evil, and rejects it.

$$\star \quad \star \quad \star$$

Cordelia, Kent, Edgar, the Fool – these form a group not less remarkable than that which we have just left. There is in the world of *King Lear* the same abundance of extreme good as of extreme evil. It generates in profusion selfless devotion and unconquerable love. And the strange thing is that neither Shakespeare nor we are surprised. We approve these characters, admire them, love them; but we feel no mystery. We do not ask in bewilderment, Is there any cause in nature that makes these kind hearts? . . . Yet surely, if we condemn the universe for Cordelia's death, we ought also to remember that it gave her birth. . . .

Of these four characters Edgar excites the least enthusiasm, but he is the one whose development is the most marked. His behaviour in the early part of the play, granted that it is not too improbable, is so foolish as to provoke one. But he learns by experience, and becomes the most capable person in the story, without losing any of his purity and nobility of mind. There remain in him, however, touches which a little chill one's feeling for him.

> The gods are just, and of our pleasant vices
> Make instruments to plague us:
> The dark and vicious place where thee he got
> Cost him his eyes:

– one wishes he had not said to his dying brother those words about their dead father. 'The gods are just' would have been enough. . . . This trait in Edgar *is* characteristic. It seems to be connected with his pronounced and conscious religiousness. He interprets everything religiously, and is speaking here from an intense conviction which overrides personal feelings. With this religiousness, on the other side, is connected his cheerful and confident endurance, and his practical helpfulness and resource. He never thinks of despairing; in the worst circumstances he is sure there is something to be done to make things better. And he is sure of this, not only from temperament, but from faith in 'the clearest gods'. He is the man on whom we are to rely at the end for the recovery and welfare of the state: and we do rely on him. . . .

Nothing can subdue in him the feeling that life is sweet and must be cherished. At his worst, misconstrued, contemned, exiled, under sentence of death, 'the lowest and most dejected thing of fortune', he keeps his head erect. The inextinguishable spirit of youth and delight is in him; he *embraces* the unsubstantial air which has blown him to the worst; for him 'the worst returns to laughter'. 'Bear free and patient thoughts,' he says to his father. His own thoughts are more than patient, they are 'free', even joyous, in spite of the tender sympathies which strive in vain to overwhelm him. This ability to feel and offer great sympathy with distress, without losing through the sympathy any elasticity or strength, is a noble quality, sometimes found in souls like Edgar's, naturally buoyant and also religious. It may even be characteristic of him that, when Lear is sinking down in death, he tries to rouse him and bring him back to life. 'Look up, my lord!' he cries. It is Kent who feels that

> he hates him,
> That would upon the rack of this tough world
> Stretch him out longer.

Kent is one of the best-loved characters in Shakespeare. He is beloved for his own sake, and also for the sake of Cordelia and of Lear. We are grateful to him because he stands up for Cordelia, and because, when she is out of sight, he constantly keeps her in our minds. And how well these two love each other we see when they meet. Yet it is not Cordelia who is dearest to Kent. His love for Lear is the passion of his life: it is his life. At the beginning he braves Lear's wrath even more for Lear's sake than Cordelia's. At the end he seems to realize Cordelia's death only as it is reflected in Lear's agony. Nor does he merely love his master passionately, as Cordelia loves her father. That word 'master', and Kent's appeal to the 'authority' he saw in the old King's face, are significant. He belongs to Lear, body and soul, as a dog does to his master and god. The King is not to him old, wayward, unreasonable, piteous: he is still terrible, grand, the king of men. Through his eyes we see the Lear of Lear's prime, whom Cordelia never saw. Kent never forgets this Lear. In the Storm-scenes, even after the King becomes insane, Kent never addresses him without the old terms of respect, 'your grace', 'my lord', 'sir'. How characteristic it is that in the scene of Lear's recovery Kent speaks to him but once: it is when the King asks 'Am I in France?' and he answers 'In your own kingdom, sir'.

In acting the part of a blunt and eccentric serving-man Kent retains much of his natural character. The eccentricity seems to be put on, but the plainness which gets him set in the stocks is but an exaggeration of his plainness in the opening scene. . . . One fact about Kent is often overlooked. He is an old man. He tells Lear that he is eight and forty, but it is clear that he is much older; not so old as his master, who was 'four-score and upward' and whom he 'loved as his father', but, one may suppose, three-score and upward. From the first scene we get this impression, and in the scene with Oswald it is repeatedly confirmed. His beard is grey. 'Ancient ruffian', 'old fellow', 'you stubborn ancient knave, you reverent braggart' – these are some of the expressions applied to him. 'Sir,' he says to Cornwall, 'I am too old to learn.' If his age is not remembered, we fail to realize the full beauty of his thoughtlessness of himself, his incessant care of the King, his light-hearted indifference to fortune or fate. We lose also some of the naturalness and pathos of his feeling that his task is nearly done. Even at the end of the Fourth Act we find him saying,

> My point and period will be thoroughly wrought
> Or well or ill, as this day's battle's fought.

[In Act V Edgar tells how Kent]

>   threw him on my father,
> Told the most piteous tale of Lear and him
> That ever ear received; which in recounting
> His grief grew puissant, and the strings of life
> Began to crack. Twice then the trumpet sounded,
> And there I left him tranced;

and a little after, when he enters, we hear the sound of death in his voice:

> I am come
> To bid my king and master aye goodnight.

This desire possesses him wholly. . . . It is of himself he is speaking, perhaps, when he murmurs, as his master dies, 'Break, heart, I prithee, break!' He puts aside Albany's invitation to take part in the government; his task is over:

> I have a journey, sir, shortly to go:
> My master calls me; I must not say no.

. . . [Kent] lives mainly by the love in his own heart.

The theatrical fool or clown (we need not distinguish them here) was a sore trial to the cultured poet and spectator in Shakespeare's day. . . . The more learned critics and poets went further and would have abolished the fool altogether. His part declines as the drama advances, diminishing markedly at the end of the sixteenth century. Jonson and Massinger exclude him. . . . But the Fool is one of Shakespeare's triumphs in *King Lear*. Imagine the tragedy without him, and you hardly know it. To remove him would spoil its harmony, as the harmony of a picture would be spoiled if one of the colours were extracted. . . .

To suppose that the Fool is, like many a domestic fool at that time, a perfectly sane man pretending to be half-witted, is surely a most prosaic blunder. There is no difficulty in imagining that, being slightly touched in the brain, and holding the office of fool, he performs the duties of his office intentionally as well as involuntarily: it is evident that he does so. But unless we suppose that he *is* touched in the brain we lose half the effect of his appearance in the Storm-scenes. . . . The insanity of the King differs from that of the beggar not only in its nature, but also in the fact that one is real and the other simply a pretence. Are we to suppose then that the insanity of the third character, the Fool, is, in this respect, a mere repetition of that of the second, the beggar – that it too is *mere* pretence? To suppose this is not only to impoverish miserably the impression made by the trio as a whole, it is also to diminish the heroic and pathetic effect of the character of the Fool. For his heroism consists largely in this, that his efforts to outjest his master's injuries are the efforts of a being to whom a responsible and consistent course of action, nay even a responsible use of language, is at the best of times difficult, and from whom it is never at the best of times expected. It is a heroism something like that of Lear himself in his endeavour to learn patience at the age of eighty. . . .

Another question [is] whether the Fool is a man or a boy. Here the evidence and the grounds for discussion are more tangible. He is frequently addressed as 'boy'. This is not decisive; but Lear's first words to him, 'How now, my pretty knave, how dost thou?' are difficult to reconcile with the idea of his being a man, and the use of this phrase on his first entrance may show Shakespeare's desire to prevent any mistake on the point. As a boy, too, he would be more strongly contrasted in the Storm-scenes with Edgar as well as with Lear; his faithfulness and courage would be even more heroic and touching; his devotion to Cordelia, and the consequent bitterness of some of his speeches to Lear, would be even more natural. . . . He pines away when Cordelia goes to France. Though he takes great liberties with his master he is frightened by Goneril, and becomes quite silent when the quarrel rises high. In the terrible scene between Lear and his two daughters and Cornwall (II.iv.129–289), he says not a word; we have almost forgotten his presence when, at the topmost pitch of passion, Lear suddenly turns to him from the hateful faces that encompass him:

> You think I'll weep;
> No, I'll not weep:
> I have full cause of weeping; but this heart
> Shall break into a hundred thousand flaws
> Or ere I'll weep. O fool, I shall go mad.

From the beginning of the Storm-scenes, though he thinks of his master alone, we perceive from his words that the cold and rain are almost more than he can bear. His childishness comes home to us when he runs out of the hovel, terrified by the madman and crying out to the King 'Help me, help me', and the good Kent takes him by the hand and draws him to his side. A little later he exclaims, 'This cold night will turn us all to fools and madmen'; and almost from that point he leaves the King to Edgar, speaking only once again in the remaining hundred lines of the scene. In the shelter of the 'farm-house' (III.vi.) he revives, and resumes his office of love; but . . . when, a little later, the King is being carried away on a litter, the Fool sits idle. He is so benumbed and worn out that he scarcely notices what is going on. Kent has to rouse him with the words,

> Come, help to bear thy master,
> Thou must not stay behind.

We know no more [and] it seems strange indeed that Shakespeare should have left us thus in ignorance. But we have seen that there are many marks of haste and carelessness in *King Lear*, and it may also be observed that, if the poet imagined the Fool dying on the way to Dover of the effects of that night upon the heath, he could perhaps convey this idea to the audience by instructing the actor who took the part to show, as he left the stage for the last time, the recognized tokens of approaching death.

Something has now been said of the four characters, Lear, Edgar, Kent and the Fool, who are together in the storm upon the heath. . . . These scenes, as we observed, suggest the idea of a convulsion in which Nature herself joins with the forces of evil in man to overpower the weak; and they are thus one of the main sources of the more terrible impressions produced by *King Lear*. But they have at the same time an effect of a totally different kind, because in them are exhibited also the strength and the beauty of Lear's nature, and, in Kent and the Fool and Edgar, the ideal of faithful devoted love. Hence from the beginning to the end of these scenes we have, mingled with pain and awe and a sense of man's infirmity, an equally strong feeling of his greatness; and this becomes at times even an exulting sense of the powerlessness of outward calamity or the malice of others against his soul. And this is one reason why imagination and emotion are never here pressed painfully inward, as in the scenes between Lear and his daughters, but are liberated and dilated. □

When considering these characters Bradley nowhere questions the rights and wrongs of their social status or the possibility of freedom from those restraints, and so, with Cordelia, the one reserved for last, interest is centred on her affections, moral qualities, reticent speech (see pp. 25–6, above), and personal destiny, not her royal status and political responsibilities.

■ The character of Cordelia is not a masterpiece of invention or subtlety like that of Cleopatra; yet in its own way it is a creation as wonderful. Cordelia appears in only four of the twenty-six scenes of *King Lear*; she speaks – it is hard to believe it – scarcely more than a hundred lines; and yet no character in Shakespeare is more absolutely individual or more ineffaceably stamped on the memory of his readers. There is a harmony, strange but perhaps the result of intention, between the character itself and this reserved or parsimonious method of depicting it. An expressiveness almost inexhaustible gained through paucity of expression; the suggestion of infinite wealth and beauty conveyed by the very refusal to reveal this beauty in expansive speech – this is at once the nature of Cordelia herself and the chief characteristic of Shakespeare's art in representing it. . . .

Cordelia's hatred of hypocrisy and of the faintest appearance of mercenary professions reminds us of Isabella's hatred of impurity [in *Measure for Measure*]; but Cordelia's position is infinitely more difficult, and on the other hand there is mingled with her hatred a touch of personal antagonism and of pride. Lear's words,

> Let pride, which she calls plainness, marry her!

are monstrously unjust, but they contain one grain of truth; and indeed it was scarcely possible that a nature so strong as Cordelia's, and with so keen a sense of dignity, should feel here nothing whatever of pride and resentment. This side of her character is emphatically shown in her language to her sisters in the first scene – language perfectly just, but little adapted to soften their hearts towards their father – and again in the very last words we hear her speak. She and her father are brought in, prisoners, to the enemy's camp; but she sees only Edmund, not those 'greater' ones on whose pleasure hangs her father's fate and her own. For her own she is little concerned; she knows how to meet adversity:

> For thee, oppressed king, am I cast down;
> Myself could else out-frown false fortune's frown.

. . . Then, after those austere words about fortune, she suddenly asks,

> Shall we not see these daughters and these sisters?

Strange last words for us to hear from a being so worshipped and beloved; but how characteristic! Their tone is unmistakable. I doubt if she could have brought herself to plead with her sisters for her father's life; and if she had attempted the task, she would have performed it but ill. Nor is our feeling towards her altered one whit by that. But what is true of Kent and the Fool is, in its measure, true of her. Any one of them would gladly have died a hundred deaths to help King Lear; and they do help his soul; but they harm his cause. They are all involved in tragedy.

Why does Cordelia die? I suppose no reader ever failed to ask that question . . . in bewilderment or dismay, and even perhaps in tones of protest. These feelings are probably evoked more strongly here than at the death of any other notable character in Shakespeare; and it may sound a wilful paradox to assert that the slightest element of reconciliation is mingled with them or succeeds them. Yet it seems to me indubitable that such an element is present, though difficult to make out with certainty what it is or whence it proceeds. . . . It is not due, or is due only in some slight degree, to a perception that the event is true to life. . . . This destruction of the good through the evil of others is one of the tragic facts of life, and no one can object to the use of it,

within certain limits, in tragic art. . . . Nevertheless the touch of reconciliation that we feel in contemplating the death of Cordelia is not due,
or is due only in some slight degree, to a perception that the event is
true to life, admissible in tragedy, and a case of a law which we cannot
seriously desire to see abrogated.

What then is this feeling, and whence does it come? I believe that
we shall find that it is a feeling not confined to *King Lear*, but present
at the close of other tragedies; and that the reason why it has an exceptional tone or force at the close of *King Lear*, lies in that very peculiarity of the close which also – at least for the moment – excites
bewilderment, dismay, or protest. The feeling I mean is the impression
that the heroic being, though in one sense and outwardly he has failed,
is yet in another sense superior to the world in which he appears; is, in
some way which we do not seek to define, untouched by the doom that
overtakes him; and is rather set free from life than deprived of it. . . . It
is simply the feeling that what happens to such a being does not matter;
all that matters is what she is. How this can be when, for anything the
tragedy tells us, she has ceased to exist, we do not ask; but the tragedy
itself makes us feel that somehow it is so. And the force with which this
impression is conveyed depends largely on the very fact which excites
our bewilderment and protest, that her death, following on the deaths
of all the evil characters, and brought about by an unexplained delay in
Edmund's effort to save her, comes on us, not as an inevitable conclusion to the sequence of events, but as the sudden stroke of mere fate or
chance. The force of the impression, that is to say, depends on the very
violence of the contrast between the outward and the inward, Cordelia's
death and Cordelia's soul. The more unmotived, unmerited, senseless,
monstrous, her fate, the more do we feel that it does not concern her.
The extremity of the disproportion between prosperity and goodness
first shocks us, and then flashes on us the conviction that our whole attitude in asking or expecting that goodness should be prosperous is
wrong; that, if only we could see things as they are, we should see that
the outward is nothing and the inward is all.

And some such thought as this (which, to bring it clearly out, I have
stated, and still state, in a form both exaggerated and much too
explicit) is really present through the whole play. Whether
Shakespeare knew it or not, it is present. I might almost say that the
'moral' of *King Lear* is presented in the irony of this collocation:

> *Albany.*   The gods defend her!
> *Enter Lear with Cordelia dead in his arms.*

The 'gods', it seems, do *not* show their approval by 'defending' their
own from adversity or death, or by giving them power and prosperity.

These, on the contrary, are worthless, or worse; it is not on them, but on the renunciation of them, that the gods throw incense. They breed lust, pride, hardness of heart, the insolence of office, cruelty, scorn, hypocrisy, contention, war, murder, self-destruction. The whole story beats this indictment of prosperity into the brain. . . .

This, if we like to use the word, is Shakespeare's 'pessimism' in *King Lear*. As we have seen, it is not by any means the whole spirit of the tragedy, which presents the world as a place where heavenly good grows side by side with evil, where extreme evil cannot long endure, and where all that survives the storm is good, if not great. But still this strain of thought, to which the world appears as the kingdom of evil and therefore worthless, is in the tragedy. . . . Pursued further and allowed to dominate, it would destroy the tragedy; for it is necessary to tragedy that we should feel that suffering and death do matter greatly, and that happiness and life are not to be renounced as worthless. Pursued further, again, it leads to the idea that the world, in that obvious appearance of it which tragedy cannot dissolve without dissolving itself, is illusive. And its tendency towards this idea is traceable in *King Lear*, in the shape of the notion that this 'great world' is transitory, or 'will wear out to nought' like the little world called 'man' (IV.vi.137), or that humanity will destroy itself.   (pp. 222–49) □

CHAPTER ELEVEN

Macbeth

■ The other three tragedies all open with conversations which lead into the action: here the action bursts into wild life amidst the sounds of a thunderstorm and the echoes of a distant battle. It hurries through seven very brief scenes of mounting suspense to a terrible crisis, which is reached, in the murder of Duncan, at the beginning of the Second Act. Pausing a moment and changing its shape, it hastes again with scarcely diminished speed to fresh horrors. And even when the speed of the outward action is slackened, the same effect is continued in another form: we are shown a soul tortured by an agony which admits not a moment's repose, and rushing in frenzy towards its doom. *Macbeth* is very much shorter than the other three tragedies, but our experience in traversing it is so crowded and intense that it leaves an impression not of brevity but of speed. It is the most vehement, the most concentrated, perhaps we may say the most tremendous, of the tragedies. . . .

[The] darkness, the lights and colours that illuminate it, the storm that rushes through it, [and] violent and gigantic images [see pp. 8–11, above] [all] conspire with the appearances of the Witches and the Ghost to awaken horror, and in some degree also a supernatural dread. And to this effect other influences contribute. The pictures called up by the mere words of the Witches stir the same feelings – those, for example, of the spell-bound sailor driven tempest-tost for nine times nine weary weeks, and never visited by sleep night or day; of the drop of poisonous foam that forms on the moon, and, falling to earth, is collected for pernicious ends; of the sweltering venom of the toad, the finger of the babe killed at its birth by its own mother, the tricklings from the murderer's gibbet. In Nature, again, something is felt to be at work, sympathetic with human guilt and supernatural malice. She labours with portents.

Lamentings heard in the air, strange screams of death,
And prophesying with accents terrible,

burst from her. The owl clamours all through the night; Duncan's horses devour each other in frenzy; the dawn comes, but no light with it. Common sights and sounds, the crying of crickets, the croak of the raven, the light thickening after sunset, the home-coming of the rooks, are all ominous. Then, as if to deepen these impressions, Shakespeare has concentrated attention on the obscurer regions of man's being, on phenomena which make it seem that he is in the power of secret forces lurking below, and independent of his consciousness and will: such as the relapse of Macbeth from conversation into a reverie, during which he gazes fascinated at the image of murder drawing closer and closer; the writing on his face of strange things he never meant to show; the pressure of imagination heightening into illusion, like the vision of a dagger in the air, at first bright, then suddenly splashed with blood, or the sound of a voice that cried 'Sleep no more' and would not be silenced. To these are added other, and constant, allusions to sleep, man's strange half-conscious life; to the misery of its withholding; to the terrible dreams of remorse; to the cursed thoughts from which Banquo is free by day, but which tempt him in his sleep: and again to abnormal disturbances of sleep; in the two men, of whom one during the murder of Duncan laughed in his sleep, and the other raised a cry of murder; and in Lady Macbeth, who rises to re-enact in somnambulism those scenes the memory of which is pushing her on to madness or suicide. All this has one effect, to excite supernatural alarm and, even more, a dread of the presence of evil not only in its recognized seat but all through and around our mysterious nature. Perhaps there is no other work equal to *Macbeth* in the production of this effect.

It is enhanced – to take a last point – by the use of a literary expedient. Not even in *Richard III*, which in this, as in other respects, has resemblances to *Macbeth*, is there so much of Irony. I do not refer to irony in the ordinary sense; to speeches, for example, where the speaker is intentionally ironical, like that of Lennox in III.vi. I refer to irony on the part of the author himself, to ironical juxtapositions of persons and events, and especially to the 'Sophoclean irony' by which a speaker is made to use words bearing to the audience, in addition to his own meaning, a further and ominous sense, hidden from himself and, usually, from the other persons on the stage. The very first words uttered by Macbeth,

So foul and fair a day I have not seen,

are an example to which attention has often been drawn; for they startle the reader by recalling the words of the Witches in the first scene,

Fair is foul, and foul is fair.

When Macbeth, emerging from his murderous reverie, turns to the nobles saying, 'Let us toward the King', his words are innocent, but to the reader have a double meaning. Duncan's comment on the treachery of Cawdor,

> There's no art
> To find the mind's construction in the face:
> He was a gentleman on whom I built
> An absolute trust,

is interrupted by the entrance of the traitor Macbeth, who is greeted with effusive gratitude and a like 'absolute trust'. . . . To the reader [familiar with the text] Lady Macbeth's light words,

> A little water clears us of this deed:
> How easy is it then,

summon up the picture of the sleep-walking scene. The idea of the Porter's speech, in which he imagines himself the keeper of hell-gate, shows the same irony. So does the contrast between the obvious and the hidden meanings of the apparitions of the armed head, the bloody child, and the child with the tree in his hand. It would be easy to add further examples. Perhaps the most striking is the answer which Banquo, as he rides away, never to return alive, gives to Macbeth's reminder, 'Fail not our feast'. 'My lord, I will not,' he replies, and he keeps his promise. It cannot be by accident that Shakespeare so frequently in this play uses a device which contributes to excite the vague fear of hidden forces operating on minds unconscious of their influence.   (pp. 253–8) □

Having considered the over-arching atmosphere of the tragedy Bradley examines a number of views that were current at that time about the nature of the Witches and their influence on the play's action. He concludes:

■ The Witches and their prophecies, if they are to be rationalized or taken symbolically, must represent not only the evil slumbering in the hero's soul, but all those obscurer influences of the evil around him in the world which aid his own ambition and the incitements of his wife. Such influences, even if we put aside all belief in evil 'spirits', are as certain, momentous, and terrifying facts as the presence of inchoate evil in the soul itself; and if we exclude all reference to these facts from our idea of the Witches, it will be greatly impoverished and will certainly fail to correspond with the imaginative effect. . . . The words of the Witches are fatal to the hero only because there is in him something which leaps into light at the sound of them; but they are at the same time the witness of forces which never cease to work in the world around him, and, on the instant of his surrender to them, entangle him inextricably in the web of Fate. If the inward connection is once realized (and Shakespeare has left us no excuse for missing it), we need not fear, and indeed shall scarcely be able, to exaggerate the effect of the Witch-scenes in heightening and deepening the sense of fear, horror, and mystery which pervades the atmosphere of the tragedy. (pp. 264–5) □

With this preparation, Bradley turns to the two leading characters, what they say and do, and, characteristically, emphasizes both their inner consciousness and their physical reactions.

■ From this murky background stand out the two great terrible figures, who dwarf all the remaining characters of the drama. Both are sublime, and both inspire, far more than the other tragic heroes, the feeling of awe. They are never detached in imagination from the atmosphere which surrounds them and adds to their grandeur and terror. It is, as it were, continued into their souls. For within them is all that we felt without – the darkness of night, lit with the flame of tempest and the hues of blood, and haunted by wild and direful shapes, 'murdering ministers', spirits of remorse, and maddening visions of peace lost and judgment to come. The way to be untrue to Shakespeare here, as always, is to relax the tension of imagination, to conventionalize, to conceive Macbeth, for example, as a half-hearted cowardly criminal, and Lady Macbeth as a whole-hearted fiend.

These two characters are fired by one and the same passion of ambition; and to a considerable extent they are alike. The disposition of each is high, proud, and commanding. They are born to rule, if not to reign. They are peremptory or contemptuous to their inferiors. They are not children of light, like Brutus and Hamlet; they are of the world. We observe in them no love of country, and no interest in the welfare of anyone outside their family. Their habitual thoughts and aims are, and, we imagine, long have been, all of station and power. And though in both there is something, and in one much, of what is higher – honour, conscience, humanity – they do not live consciously in the light of these things or speak their language. Not that they are egoists, like Iago; or, if they are egoists, theirs is an *egoïsme à deux*. They have no separate ambitions. They support and love one another. They suffer together. And if, as time goes on, they drift a little apart, they are not vulgar souls, to be alienated and recriminate when they experience the fruitlessness of their ambition. They remain to the end tragic, even grand.

So far there is much likeness between them. Otherwise they are contrasted, and the action is built upon this contrast. Their attitudes towards the projected murder of Duncan are quite different; and it produces in them equally different effects. In consequence, they appear in the earlier part of the play as of equal importance, if indeed Lady Macbeth does not overshadow her husband; but afterwards she retires more and more into the background, and he becomes unmistakably the leading figure. His is indeed far the more complex character: and I will speak of it first.

Macbeth, the cousin of a King mild, just, and beloved, but now too old to lead his army, is introduced to us as a general of extraordinary prowess, who has covered himself with glory in putting down a rebellion and repelling the invasion of a foreign army. In these conflicts he showed great personal courage, a quality which he continues to display throughout the drama in regard to all plain dangers. It is difficult to be sure of his customary demeanour, for in the play we see him either in what appears to be an exceptional relation to his wife, or else in the throes of remorse and desperation; but from his behaviour during his journey home after the war, from his *later* conversations with Lady Macbeth, and from his language to the murderers of Banquo and to others, we imagine him as a great warrior, somewhat masterful, rough, and abrupt, a man to inspire some fear and much admiration. He was thought 'honest', or honourable; he was trusted, apparently, by everyone; Macduff, a man of the highest integrity, 'loved him well'. And there was, in fact, much good in him. We have no warrant, I think, for describing him, with many writers, as of a 'noble' nature, like Hamlet or Othello; but he had a keen sense both of humour and of the worth of a good name. The phrase, again, 'too full of the milk of human kindness', is applied to him in impatience by his wife, who did not fully understand him; but certainly he was far from devoid of humanity and pity.

At the same time he was exceedingly ambitious. He must have been so by temper. The tendency must have been greatly strengthened by his marriage. When we see him, it has been further stimulated by his remarkable success and by the consciousness of exceptional powers and merit. It becomes a passion. The course of action suggested by it is extremely perilous: it sets his good name, his position, and even his life on the hazard. It is also abhorrent to his better feelings. Their defeat in the struggle with ambition leaves him utterly wretched, and would have kept him so, however complete had been his outward success and security. On the other hand, his passion for power and his instinct of self-assertion are so vehement that no inward misery could persuade him to relinquish the fruits of crime, or to advance from remorse to repentance.

In the character as so far sketched there is nothing very peculiar, though the strength of the forces contending in it is unusual. But there is in Macbeth one marked peculiarity, the true apprehension of which is the key to Shakespeare's conception. This bold ambitious man of action, has, within certain limits, the imagination of a poet – an imagination on the one hand extremely sensitive to impressions of a certain kind, and, on the other, productive of violent disturbance both of mind and body. Through it he is kept in contact with supernatural impressions and is liable to supernatural fears. And through it, especially, come to him the intimations of conscience and honour. Macbeth's better nature – to put the matter for clearness' sake too broadly – instead of speaking to him in the overt language of moral ideas, commands, and prohibitions, incorporates itself in images which alarm and horrify. His imagination is thus the best of him, something usually deeper and higher than his conscious thoughts; and if he had obeyed it he would have been safe. But his wife quite misunderstands it, and he himself understands it only in part. The terrifying images which deter him from crime and follow its commission, and which are really the protest of his deepest self, seem to his wife the creations of mere nervous fear, and are sometimes referred by himself to the dread of vengeance or the restlessness of insecurity. His conscious or reflective mind, that is, moves chiefly among considerations of outward success and failure, while his inner being is convulsed by conscience. And his inability to understand himself is repeated and exaggerated in the interpretations of actors and critics, who represent him as a coward, cold-blooded, calculating, and pitiless, who shrinks from crime simply because it is dangerous, and suffers afterwards simply because he is not safe. In reality his courage is frightful. He strides from crime to crime, though his soul never ceases to bar his advance with shapes of terror, or to clamour in his ears that he is murdering his peace and casting away his 'eternal jewel'.

It is of the first importance to realize the strength, and also (what has not been so clearly recognized) the limits, of Macbeth's imagination. It is not the universal meditative imagination of Hamlet. He came to see in man, as Hamlet sometimes did, the 'quintessence of dust'; but he must always have been incapable of Hamlet's reflections on man's noble reason and infinite faculty, or of seeing with Hamlet's eyes 'this brave o'erhanging firmament, this majestical roof fretted with golden fire'. Nor could he feel, like Othello, the romance of war or the infinity of love. He shows no sign of any unusual sensitiveness to the glory or beauty in the world or the soul; and it is partly for this reason that we have no inclination to love him, and that we regard him with more of awe than of pity. His imagination is excitable and intense, but narrow. That which stimulates it is, almost solely, that which thrills

even brutal, or he becomes a cool pitiless hypocrite. He is generally said to be a very bad actor, but this is not wholly true. Whenever his imagination stirs, he acts badly. It so possesses him, and is so much stronger than his reason, that his face betrays him, and his voice utters the most improbable untruths or the most artificial rhetoric. But when it is asleep he is firm, self-controlled and practical, as in the conversation where he skilfully elicits from Banquo that information about his movements which is required for the successful arrangement of his murder. . . .

[Macbeth] himself feels with such intensity the enormity of his purpose that, it seems clear, neither his ambition nor yet the prophecy of the Witches would ever without the aid of Lady Macbeth have overcome this feeling. As it is, the deed is done in horror and without the faintest desire or sense of glory – done, one may almost say, as if it were an appalling duty; and, the instant it is finished, its futility is revealed to Macbeth as clearly as its vileness had been revealed beforehand. As he staggers from the scene he mutters in despair,

> Wake Duncan with thy knocking! I would thou could'st.

When, half an hour later, he returns with Lennox from the room of the murder, he breaks out:

> Had I but died an hour before this chance,
> I had lived a blessed time; for from this instant
> There's nothing serious in mortality:
> All is but toys: renown and grace is dead;
> The wine of life is drawn, and the mere lees
> Is left this vault to brag of.

This is no mere acting. The language here has none of the false rhetoric of his merely hypocritical speeches. It is meant to deceive, but it utters at the same time his profoundest feeling. And this he can henceforth never hide from himself for long. However he may try to drown it in further enormities, he hears it murmuring,

> Duncan is in his grave:
> After life's fitful fever he sleeps well:

or,

> better be with the dead:

or,

> I have lived long enough:

and it speaks its last words on the last day of his life:

Out, out, brief candle!
Life's but a walking shadow, a poor player
That struts and frets his hour upon the stage
And then is heard no more: it is a tale
Told by an idiot, full of sound and fury,
Signifying nothing. . . .

The history of Macbeth after the murder of Duncan. . . . excites little suspense or anxiety on his account: we have now no hope for him. But it is an engrossing spectacle. . . . That heart-sickness which comes from Macbeth's perception of the futility of his crime, and which never leaves him for long, is not, however, his habitual state. It could not be so, for two reasons. In the first place the consciousness of guilt is stronger in him than the consciousness of failure; and it keeps him in a perpetual agony of restlessness, and forbids him simply to droop and pine. His mind is 'full of scorpions'. He cannot sleep. He 'keeps alone', moody and savage. 'All that is within him does condemn itself for being there.' There is a fever in his blood which urges him to ceaseless action in the search for oblivion. And, in the second place, ambition, the love of power, the instinct of self-assertion, are much too potent in Macbeth to permit him to resign, even in spirit, the prize for which he has put rancours in the vessel of his peace. The 'will to live' is mighty in him. The forces which impelled him to aim at the crown re-assert themselves. He faces the world, and his own conscience, desperate, but never dreaming of acknowledging defeat. He will see 'the frame of things disjoint' first. He challenges fate into the lists.

The result is frightful. He speaks no more, as before Duncan's murder, of honour or pity. That sleepless torture, he tells himself, is nothing but the sense of insecurity and the fear of retaliation. If only he were safe, it would vanish. And he looks about for the cause of his fear; and his eye falls on Banquo. Banquo, who cannot fail to suspect him, has not fled or turned against him: Banquo has become his chief counsellor. Why? Because, he answers, the kingdom was promised to Banquo's children. Banquo, then, is waiting to attack him, to make a way for them. The 'bloody instructions' he himself taught when he murdered Duncan, are about to return, as he said they would, to plague the inventor. *This* then, he tells himself, is the fear that will not let him sleep; and it will die with Banquo. There is no hesitation now, and no remorse: he has nearly learned his lesson. He hastens feverishly, not to murder Banquo, but to procure his murder: some strange idea is in his mind that the thought of the dead man will not haunt him, like the memory of Duncan, if the deed is done by other hands. The deed is done: but, instead of peace descending on him, from the depths of his nature his half-murdered conscience rises; his deed confronts

spoken as they are by a man already in some measure prepared for such news, and now transported by the frenzy of his last fight for life. He has no time now to feel. Only, as he thinks of the morrow when time to feel will come – if anything comes – the vanity of all hopes and forward-lookings sinks deep into his soul with an infinite weariness, and he murmurs,

> To-morrow, and to-morrow, and to-morrow,
> Creeps in this petty pace from day to day
> To the last syllable of recorded time,
> And all our yesterdays have lighted fools
> The way to dusty death.

In the very depths a gleam of his native love of goodness, and with it a touch of tragic grandeur, rests upon him. The evil he has desperately embraced continues to madden or to wither his inmost heart. No experience in the world could bring him to glory in it or make his peace with it, or to forget what he once was and Iago and Goneril never were.   (pp. 265–79)   □

A return to the start of the play and one of Bradley's most sustained accounts of 'character' concentrates attention on Lady Macbeth's contribution to the play's action:

■ The first half of *Macbeth* is greater than the second, and in the first half Lady Macbeth not only appears more than in the second but exerts the ultimate deciding influence on the action. . . . Sharing . . . certain traits with her husband, she is at once clearly distinguished from him by an inflexibility of will, which appears to hold imagination, feeling, and conscience completely in check. To her the prophecy of things that will be becomes instantaneously the determination that they shall be:

> Glamis thou art, and Cawdor, and shalt be
> What thou art promised.

She knows her husband's weakness, how he scruples 'to catch the nearest way' to the object he desires; and she sets herself without a trace of doubt or conflict to counteract this weakness. To her there is no separation between will and deed; and, as the deed falls in part to her, she is sure it will be done:

> The raven himself is hoarse
> That croaks the fatal entrance of Duncan
> Under my battlements.

On the moment of Macbeth's rejoining her, after braving infinite dangers and winning infinite praise, without a syllable on these subjects or a word of affection, she goes straight to her purpose and permits him to speak of nothing else. She takes the superior position and assumes the direction of affairs – appears to assume it even more than she really can, that she may spur him on. She animates him by picturing the deed as heroic, 'this night's *great* business', or 'our *great* quell', while she ignores its cruelty and faithlessness. She bears down his faint resistance by presenting him with a prepared scheme which may remove from him the terror and danger of deliberation. She rouses him with a taunt no man can bear, and least of all a soldier – the word 'coward'. She appeals even to his love for her:

> from this time
> Such I account thy love;

– such, that is, as the protestations of a drunkard. Her seasonings are mere sophisms; they could persuade no man. It is not by them, it is by personal appeals, through the admiration she extorts from him, and through sheer force of will, that she impels him to the deed. Her eyes are fixed upon the crown and the means to it; she does not attend to the consequences. Her plan of laying the guilt upon the chamberlains is invented on the spur of the moment, and simply to satisfy her husband. Her true mind is heard in the ringing cry with which she answers his question, 'Will it not be received . . . that they have done it?'

> Who *dares* receive it other?

And this is repeated in the sleep-walking scene: 'What need we fear who knows it, when none can call our power to account?' Her passionate courage sweeps him off his feet. His decision is taken in a moment of enthusiasm:

> Bring forth men-children only;
> For thy undaunted mettle should compose
> Nothing but males.

And even when passion has quite died away her will remains supreme. In presence of overwhelming horror and danger, in the murder scene and the banquet scene, her self-control is perfect. When the truth of what she has done dawns on her, no word of complaint, scarcely a word of her own suffering, not a single word of her own as apart from his, escapes her when others are by. She helps him, but never asks his

and during it, are heard by her as simple facts, and are referred to their true sources. The knocking has no mystery for her: it comes from 'the south entry'. She calculates on the drunkenness of the grooms, compares the different effects of wine on herself and on them, and listens to their snoring. To her the blood upon her husband's hands suggests only the taunt,

> My hands are of your colour, but I shame
> To wear a heart so white;

and the blood to her is merely 'this filthy witness' – words impossible to her husband, to whom it suggested something quite other than sensuous disgust or practical danger. The literalism of her mind appears fully in two contemptuous speeches where she dismisses his imaginings; in the murder scene:

> Infirm of purpose!
> Give me the daggers! The sleeping and the dead
> Are but as pictures: 'tis the eye of childhood
> That fears a painted devil;

and in the banquet scene:

> O these flaws and starts,
> Impostors to true fear, would well become
> A woman's story at a winter's fire,
> Authorised by her grandam. Shame itself!
> Why do you make such faces? When all's done,
> You look but on a stool.

Even in the awful scene where her imagination breaks loose in sleep she uses no such images as Macbeth's. It is the direct appeal of the facts to sense that has fastened on her memory. The ghastly realism of 'Yet who would have thought the old man to have had so much blood in him?' or 'Here's the smell of the blood still', is wholly unlike him. Her most poetical words, 'All the perfumes of Arabia will not sweeten this little hand', are equally unlike his words about great Neptune's ocean. Hers, like some of her other speeches, are the more moving from their greater simplicity ... The quality which moves our admiration is courage or force of will.

This want of imagination, though it helps to make Lady Macbeth strong for immediate action, is fatal to her. ... [The] facile realism [of], 'A little water clears us of this deed' will one day be answered by herself, 'Will these hands ne'er be clean?' ... the fatal commonplace,

'What's done is done', will make way for her last despairing sentence, 'What's done cannot be undone'.

Hence the development of her character – perhaps it would be more strictly accurate to say, the change in her state of mind – is both inevitable, and the opposite of the development we traced in Macbeth. When the murder has been done, the discovery of its hideousness, first reflected in the faces of her guests, comes to Lady Macbeth with the shock of a sudden disclosure, and at once her nature begins to sink. The first intimation of the change is given when, in the scene of the discovery, she faints. When next we see her, Queen of Scotland, the glory of her dream has faded. She enters, disillusioned, and weary with want of sleep: she has thrown away everything and gained nothing:

> Nought's had, all's spent,
> Where our desire is got without content:
> 'Tis safer to be that which we destroy
> Than by destruction dwell in doubtful joy.

Henceforth she has no initiative: the stem of her being seems to be cut through. Her husband, physically the stronger, maddened by pangs he had foreseen, but still flaming with life, comes into the foreground. . . . In the sudden emergency of the banquet scene she makes a prodigious and magnificent effort; her strength, and with it her ascendancy, returns, and she saves her husband at least from an open disclosure. But after this she takes no part whatever in the action. We only know from her shuddering words in the sleep-walking scene, 'The Thane of Fife had a wife: where is she now?' that she has even learned of her husband's worst crime; and in all the horrors of his tyranny over Scotland she has, so far as we hear, no part. . . . She sinks slowly downward. She cannot bear darkness, and has light by her continually: 'tis her command. At last her nature, not her will, gives way. The secrets of the past find vent in a disorder of sleep, the beginning perhaps of madness. . . . Her death is announced by a cry from her women so sudden and direful that it would thrill her husband with horror if he were any longer capable of fear. In the last words of the play Malcolm tells us it is believed in the hostile army that she died by her own hand.   (pp. 280–8)

★　★　★

Banquo being at first strongly contrasted with Macbeth, as an innocent man with a guilty, . . . may be described much more truly than Macbeth as the victim of the Witches. . . . On hearing the predictions concerning himself and his descendants he makes no answer, and when

story, if truly apprehended, produces this impression quite as strongly as the more terrific stories of the chief characters, and perhaps even more clearly, inasmuch as he is nearer to average human nature, has obviously at first a quiet conscience, and uses with evident sincerity the language of religion.   (pp. 290–6) □

Apart from his story, Bradley found Banquo's character neither 'very interesting' *nor* 'perfectly individual' *and he viewed other* 'minor characters' *in much the same way*:

■ They are sketched lightly, and are seldom developed further than the strict purposes of the action required. From this point of view they are inferior to several of the less important figures in each of the other three tragedies. The scene in which Lady Macduff and her child appear, and the passage where their slaughter is reported to Macduff, have much dramatic value, but in neither case is the effect due to any great extent to the special characters of the persons concerned. Neither they, nor Duncan, nor Malcolm, nor even Banquo himself, have been imagined intensely, and therefore they do not produce that sense of unique personality which Shakespeare could convey in a much smaller number of lines than he gives to most of them. And this is of course even more the case with persons like Ross, Angus, and Lennox, though each of these has distinguishable features. . . . Let the reader turn, for instance, to the second scene of the Fifth Act, and ask himself why the names of the persons should not be interchanged in all the ways mathematically possible. Can he find, again, any signs of character by which to distinguish the speeches of Ross and Angus in Act I, scenes ii and iii, or to determine that Malcolm must have spoken I.iv.2–11? Most of this writing, we may almost say, is simply Shakespeare's writing, not that of Shakespeare become another person. . . .

Is it possible to guess the reason of this characteristic of *Macbeth*? I cannot believe it is due to the presence of a second hand. The writing, mangled by the printer and perhaps by 'the players', seems to be sometimes obviously Shakespeare's, sometimes sufficiently Shakespearean to repel any attack not based on external evidence. It may be, as the shortness of the play has suggested to some, that Shakespeare was hurried, and, throwing all his weight on the principal characters, did not exert himself in dealing with the rest. But there is another possibility which may be worth considering. *Macbeth* is distinguished by its simplicity – by grandeur in simplicity, no doubt, but still by simplicity. The two great figures indeed can hardly be called simple, except in comparison with such characters as Hamlet and Iago; but in almost every other respect the tragedy has this quality. Its plot is quite plain. It has very little intermixture of humour. It has little pathos except of the sternest kind. The style, for Shakespeare, has not much variety, being generally kept at a higher pitch than in the other three tragedies; and there is much less than usual of the interchange of verse and prose. All this makes for simplicity of effect. And, this being so, is it not possible that Shakespeare instinctively felt, or consciously feared, that to give much individuality or attraction to the subordinate figures would diminish this effect, and so, like a good artist, sacrificed a part to the whole? . . .

I would add, though without much confidence, another suggestion. The simplicity of *Macbeth* is one of the reasons why many readers feel that, in spite of its being intensely 'romantic', it is less unlike a classical tragedy than *Hamlet* or *Othello* or *King Lear*. And it is possible that this effect is, in a sense, the result of design. I do not mean that Shakespeare intended to imitate a classical tragedy; I mean only that he may have seen in the bloody story of Macbeth a subject suitable for treatment in a manner somewhat nearer to that of Seneca, or of the English Senecan plays familiar to him in his youth, than was the manner of his own mature tragedies. The Witches doubtless are 'romantic', but so is the witchcraft in Seneca's *Medea* and *Hercules Oetaeus*; indeed it is difficult to read the account of Medea's preparations (670–739) without being reminded of the incantation in *Macbeth*. Banquo's Ghost again is 'romantic', but so are Seneca's ghosts. For the swelling of the style in some of the great passages – however immeasurably superior these may be to anything in Seneca – and certainly for the turgid bombast which occasionally appears in *Macbeth* . . . Shakespeare might easily have found a model in Seneca. Did he not think that this was the high Roman manner? Does not the Sergeant's speech, as Coleridge observed, recall the style of the 'passionate speech' of the Player in *Hamlet* – a speech, be it observed, on a Roman subject? And is it entirely an accident that parallels between Seneca and Shakespeare seem to be more frequent in *Macbeth* than in any other of his undoubtedly genuine works except perhaps *Richard III*. . . . If we suppose that Shakespeare meant to give to his play a certain classical tinge, he might naturally carry out this idea in respect to the characters, as well as in other respects, by concentrating almost the whole interest on the important figures and leaving the others comparatively shadowy.

★ ★ ★

Macbeth being more simple than the other tragedies, and broader and more massive in effect, three passages in it are of great importance as securing variety in tone, and also as affording relief from the feelings excited by the Witch-scenes and the principal characters. They are the passage where the Porter appears, the conversation between Lady Macduff and her little boy, and the passage where Macduff receives the news of the slaughter of his wife and babes. Yet the first of these, we are told even by Coleridge, is unworthy of Shakespeare and is not his; and the second, with the rest of the scene which contains it, appears to be usually omitted in stage representations of *Macbeth*.

I question if either this scene or the exhibition of Macduff's grief is required to heighten our abhorrence of Macbeth's cruelty. They have a technical value in helping to give the last stage of the action the form of a conflict between Macbeth and Macduff. But their chief function is of another kind. It is to touch the heart with a sense of beauty and pathos, to open the springs of love and of tears. Shakespeare is loved for the sweetness of his humanity, and because he makes this kind of appeal with such irresistible persuasion; and the reason why *Macbeth*, though admired as much as any work of his, is scarcely loved, is that the characters who predominate cannot make this kind of appeal, and at no point are able to inspire unmingled sympathy. The two passages in question supply this want in such measure as Shakespeare thought advisable in *Macbeth*, and the play would suffer greatly from their excision. The second, on the stage, is extremely moving, and Macbeth's reception of the news of his wife's death may be intended to recall it by way of contrast. . . .

Little Macduff exemplifies most of these remarks. . . . One does not easily forget . . . his ability to defeat his mother in argument; or the deep impression she made on him when she spoke of his father as a 'traitor'; or his immediate response when he heard the murderer call his father by the same name, 'Thou liest, thou shag-haired villain.' . . . He is perhaps the only person in the tragedy who provokes a smile. I say 'perhaps', for though the anxiety of the Doctor to escape from the company of his patient's husband makes one smile, I am not sure that it was meant to.

The Porter does not make me smile: the moment is too terrific. He is grotesque; no doubt the contrast he affords is humorous as well as ghastly; I dare say the groundlings roared with laughter at his coarsest remarks. But they are not comic enough to allow one to forget for a moment what has preceded and what must follow. And I am far from complaining of this. I believe that it is what Shakespeare intended, and that he despised the groundlings if they laughed. . . . We cannot forget how the knocking that makes him grumble sounded to Macbeth, or that within a few minutes of his opening the gate Duncan will be discovered in his blood; nor can we help feeling that in pretending to be porter of hell-gate he is terribly near the truth. To give him language so humorous that it would ask us almost to lose the sense of these things would have been a fatal mistake – the kind of mistake that means want of dramatic imagination. . . . I could believe that he left 'the players' or his collaborator to write the *words* of the passage. But that anyone except the author of the scene of Duncan's murder *conceived* the passage is incredible.

★   ★   ★

The speeches of the Porter, a low comic character, are in prose. So is the letter of Macbeth to his wife. In both these cases Shakespeare follows his general rule or custom. The only other prose-speeches occur in the sleep-walking scene, and here the use of prose may seem strange. For in great tragic scenes we expect the more poetic medium of expression and this is one of the most famous of such scenes. Besides, unless I mistake, Lady Macbeth is the only one of Shakespeare's great tragic characters who on a last appearance is denied the dignity of verse.

Yet in this scene also he adheres to his custom. Somnambulism is an abnormal condition, and it is his general rule to assign prose to persons whose state of mind is abnormal. . . . Ophelia in her madness either sings snatches of songs or speaks prose. Almost all Lear's speeches, after he has become definitely insane, are in prose: where he wakes from sleep recovered, the verse returns. . . . Othello, in IV.i, speaks in verse till the moment when Iago tells him that Cassio has confessed. There follow ten lines of prose – exclamations and mutterings of bewildered horror – and he falls to the ground unconscious.

The idea underlying this custom of Shakespeare's evidently is that the regular rhythm of verse would be inappropriate where the mind is supposed to have lost its balance and to be at the mercy of chance impressions coming from without (as sometimes with Lear), or of ideas emerging from its unconscious depths and pursuing one another across its passive surface. The somnambulism of Lady Macbeth is such a condition. There is no rational connection in the sequence of images and ideas. The sight of blood on her hand, the sound of the clock striking the hour for Duncan's murder, the hesitation of her husband before that hour came, the vision of the old man in his blood, the idea of the murdered wife of Macduff, the sight of the hand again, Macbeth's 'flaws and starts' at the sight of Banquo's ghost, the smell on her hand, the washing of hands after Duncan's murder again, her husband's fear of the buried Banquo, the sound of the knocking at the gate – these possess her, one after another, in this chance order. It is not much less accidental than the order of Ophelia's ideas; the great difference is that with Ophelia total insanity has effaced or greatly weakened the emotional force of the ideas, whereas to Lady Macbeth each new image or perception comes laden with anguish. There is, again, scarcely a sign of the exaltation of disordered imagination; we are conscious rather of an intense suffering which forces its way into light against resistance, and speaks a language for the most part strikingly bare in its diction and simple in its construction. This language stands in strong contrast with that of Macbeth in the surrounding scenes, full of a feverish and almost furious excitement, and seems to express a far more desolating misery. ... All the language of poetry – even of Macbeth's poetry – seems to be touched with unreality, and these brief toneless sentences seem the only voice of truth.   (pp. 297–307) □

CHAPTER TWELVE

Antony and Cleopatra

*F*or this addition to his lectures on the four 'great' tragedies published in *Shakespearean Tragedy, Bradley emphasized the same general concepts as before* – beauty, nobility, greatness, power – *although he found that much in this text eluded these prescripts. He concludes the lecture by saying:*

■ A comparison of Shakespearean tragedies seems to prove that the tragic emotions are stirred in the fullest possible measure only when such beauty or nobility of character is displayed as commands unreserved admiration or love; or when, in default of this, the forces which move the agents, and the conflict which results from these forces, attain a terrifying and overwhelming power. The four most famous tragedies satisfy one or both of these conditions; *Antony and Cleopatra*, though a great tragedy, satisfies neither of them completely. But to say this is not to criticize it. It does not attempt to satisfy these conditions, and then fail in the attempt. It attempts something different, and succeeds as triumphantly as *Othello* itself. In doing so it gives us what no other tragedy can give and it leaves us, no less than any other, lost in astonishment at the powers which created it. (p. 305) □

Near the start of this lecture Bradley examines the play's political situation by using his tested method of analysing the text as words that express both the conscious and unconscious mind of the speaker. He is also concerned with what is not spoken, and with narrative.

■ Most of Shakespeare's tragedies are dramatic. . . . The story is not merely exciting and impressive from the movement of conflicting forces towards a terrible issue, but from time to time there come situations and events which, even apart from their bearing on this issue, appeal most powerfully to the dramatic feelings – scenes of action or passion which agitate the audience with alarm, horror, painful expectation, or absorbing sympathies and antipathies. . . . In the first three Acts of our play what is there resembling this? Almost nothing. People converse, discuss, accuse, drink together, arrange a marriage, meet and part; but they do not kill, do not even tremble or weep. We see hardly one violent movement; until the battle of Actium is over we witness scarcely any violent passion, and that battle, as it is a naval action, we do not see. . . .

[Shakespeare], with his matchless power of depicting an inward struggle, might have made this story, even where it could not furnish him with thrilling incidents, the source of powerful tragic emotion. . . . But he does no such thing till the catastrophe is near. Antony breaks away from Cleopatra without any strenuous conflict. No serious doubt of his return is permitted to agitate us. We are almost assured of it through the impression made on us by Octavius, through occasional glimpses into Antony's mind, through the absence of any doubt in Enobarbus, through scenes in Alexandria which display Cleopatra and display her irresistible. And, finally, the downward turn itself, the fatal step of Antony's return, is shown without the slightest emphasis. . . . By the very scheme of the work, therefore, tragic impressions of any great volume or depth were reserved for the last stage of the conflict; while the main interest, down to the battle of Actium, was directed to matters exceedingly interesting and even, in the wider sense, dramatic, but not overly either terrible or piteous: on the one hand, to the political aspect of the story; on the other to the personal causes which helped to make the issue inevitable. . . .

Shakespeare, I think, took little interest in the character of Octavius, and he has not made it wholly clear. . . . His Octavius is very formidable; his cold determination half paralyses Antony. . . . More than once in the wrong . . . he never admits it; he silently pushes his rival a step backward; and, when he ceases to fear, he shows contempt. He neither enjoys war nor is great in it; at first, therefore, he is anxious about the power of Pompey, and stands in need of Antony. As soon as Antony's presence has served his turn, and he has patched up a union with him and seen him safely off to Athens, he destroys first Pompey and next Lepidus. Then, dexterously using Antony's faithlessness to Octavia and excesses in the East in order to put himself in the right, he makes for his victim with admirable celerity while he is still drunk with the joy of reunion with Cleopatra. For his ends Octavius is perfectly efficient, but he is so partly from his limitations. One phrase of his is exceedingly characteristic. When Antony in rage and desperation challenges him to single combat, Octavius calls him 'the old ruffian'. There is a horrid aptness in the phrase, but it disgusts us. It is shameful in this boy, as hard and smooth as polished steel, to feel at such a time nothing of the greatness of his victim and the tragedy of his victim's fall. . . .

The doubtful point in the character is this. [In his *Life of Antonius*, Shakespeare's source for this play], Plutarch says that Octavius was reported to love his sister dearly; and Shakespeare's Octavius several times expresses such love. When, then, he proposed the marriage with Antony (for of course it was he who spoke through Agrippa), was he honest, or was he laying a trap and, in doing so, sacrificing his sister? Did he hope the marriage would really unite him with his brother-in-law; or did he merely mean it to be a source of future differences; or did he calculate that, whether it secured peace or dissension, it would in either case bring him great advantage? Shakespeare, who was quite as intelligent as his readers, must have asked himself some such question; but he may not have cared to answer it even to himself; and, in any case, he has left the actor (at least the actor in days later than his own) to choose an answer. . . .

Though the character of Octavius is neither attractive nor wholly clear, his figure is invested with a certain tragic dignity, because he is felt to be the Man of Destiny, the agent of forces against which the intentions of an individual would avail nothing. He is represented as having himself some feeling of this sort. His lament over Antony, his grief that their stars were irreconcilable, may well be genuine, though we should be surer if it were uttered in soliloquy. His austere words to Octavia again probably speak his true mind:

> Be you not troubled with the time, which drives
> O'er your content these strong necessities;
> But let determined things to destiny
> Hold unbewailed their way.

In any case the feeling of fate comes through to us. It is aided by slight touches of supernatural effect; first in the Soothsayer's warning to Antony that his genius or angel is overpowered whenever he is near Octavius; then in the strangely effective scene where Antony's soldiers, in the night before his last battle, hear music in the air or under the earth:

> 'Tis the god Hercules, whom Antony loved,
> Now leaves him.

And in the influence of this feeling in giving impressiveness to the story is added that of the immense scale and world-wide issue of the conflict. Even the distances traversed by fleets and armies enhance this effect.

And yet there seems to be something half-hearted in Shakespeare's appeal here, something even ironical in his presentation of this conflict.

Its external magnitude, like Antony's magnificence in lavishing realms and gathering the kings of the East in his support, fails to uplift or dilate the imagination. The struggle in Lear's little island seems to us to have an infinitely wider scope. It is here that we are sometimes reminded of *Troilus and Cressida*, and the cold and disenchanting light that is there cast on the Trojan War. The spectacle which he portrays leaves Shakespeare quite undazzled; he even makes it appear inwardly small. The lordship of the world, we ask ourselves, what is it worth and in what spirit do these 'world-sharers' contend for it. They are no champions of their country like Henry V. The conqueror knows not even the glory of battle. Their aims, for all we see, are as personal as if they were captains of banditti; and they are followed merely from self-interest or private attachment. The scene on Pompey's galley is full of this irony. One 'third part of the world' is carried drunk to bed. . . . Later, a short scene [III.i], totally useless to the plot and purely satiric in its purport, is slipped in to show how Ventidius fears to pursue his Parthian conquests because it is not safe for Antony's lieutenant to outdo his master. A painful sense of hollowness oppresses us. We know too well what must happen in a world so splendid, so false, and so petty. We turn for relief from the political game to those who are sure to lose it; to those who love some human being better than a prize, to Eros and Charmian and Iras; to Enobarbus, whom the world corrupts, but who has a heart that can break with shame; to the lovers who seem to us to find in death something better than their victor's life.

This presentation of the outward conflict has two results. First, it blunts our feeling of the greatness of Antony's fall from prosperity. . . . Our deeper sympathies are focused rather on Antony's heart, on the inward fall to which the enchantment of passion leads him, and the inward recovery which succeeds it. And the second result is this. The greatness of Antony and Cleopatra in their fall is so much heightened by contrast with the world they lose and the conqueror who wins it, that the positive element in the final tragic impression, the element of reconciliation, is strongly emphasized. The peculiar effect of the drama depends partly, as we have seen, on the absence of decidedly tragic scenes and events in its first half; but it depends quite as much on this emphasis. In any Shakespearean tragedy we watch some elect spirit colliding, partly through its error and defect, with a superhuman power which bears it down; and yet we feel that this spirit, even in the error and defect, rises by its greatness into ideal union with the power that overwhelms it. In some tragedies this latter feeling is relatively weak. In *Antony and Cleopatra* it is unusually strong; stronger, with some readers at least, than the fear and grief and pity with which they contemplate the tragic error and advance of doom.   (pp. 283–92) □

*The rest of the lecture is spent on establishing the greatness of the two leading char-
acters by following the play's action and quoting the words they speak as proof of their
'sublime' natures, especially at the moment of suicide.*

■ It is plain that the love of Antony and Cleopatra is destructive; that
in some way it clashes with the nature of things; that, while they are
sitting in their paradise like gods, its walls move inward and crush
them at last to death. This is no invention of moralizing critics; it is in
the play; and any one familiar with Shakespeare would expect beforehand to find it there. But then to forget because of it the other side,
to deny the name of love to this ruinous passion, to speak as though
the lovers had utterly missed the good of life, is to mutilate the tragedy
and to ignore a great part of its effect upon us. For we sympathize with
them in their passion; we feel in it the infinity there is in man; even
while we acquiesce in their defeat we are exulting in their victory; and
when they have vanished we say,

> the odds is gone,
> And there is nothing left remarkable
> Beneath the visiting moon.

Though we hear nothing from Shakespeare of the cruelty of
Plutarch's Antony, or of the misery caused by his boundless profusion,
we do not feel the hero of the tragedy to be a man of the noblest type,
like Brutus, Hamlet, or Othello. He seeks power merely for himself,
and uses it for his own pleasure. He is in some respects unscrupulous;
and, while it would be unjust to regard his marriage exactly as if it
were one in private life, we resent his treatment of Octavia, whose
character Shakespeare was obliged to leave a mere sketch, lest our
feeling for the hero and heroine should be too much chilled. Yet, for
all this, we sympathize warmly with Antony, are greatly drawn to him,
and are inclined to regard him as a noble nature half spoiled by his
time.

It is a large, open, generous, expansive nature, quite free from envy,
capable of great magnanimity, even of entire devotion. Antony is unreserved, naturally straightforward, we may almost say simple. He can
admit faults, accept advice and even reproof, take a jest against himself
with good-humour. He is courteous (to Lepidus, for example, whom
Octavius treats with cold contempt); and, though he can be exceedingly dignified, he seems to prefer a blunt though sympathetic plainness, which is one cause of the attachment of his soldiers. He has none
of the faults of the brooder, the sentimentalist, or the man of principle; his nature tends to splendid action and lusty enjoyment. But he is
neither a mere soldier nor a mere sensualist. He has imagination, the

temper of an artist who revels in abundant and rejoicing appetites, feasts his senses on the glow and richness of life, flings himself into its mirth and revelry, yet feels the poetry in all this, and is able also to put it by and be more than content with the hardships of adventure. Such a man could never have sought a crown by a murder like Macbeth's, or like Brutus, have killed on principle the man who loved him, or have lost the world for a Cressida. . . .

A man who loved power as much as thousands of insignificant people love it, would have made a sterner struggle than Antony's against his enchantment. He can hardly be said to struggle at all. . . . When he meets Cleopatra he finds his Absolute. She satisfies, nay glorifies, his whole being. She intoxicates his senses. Her wiles, her taunts, her furies and meltings, her laughter and tears, bewitch him all alike. She loves what he loves, and she surpasses him. She can drink him to his bed, out-jest his practical jokes . . . out-dazzle his own magnificence. She is his play-fellow, and yet a great queen. Angling in the river, playing billiards, flourishing the sword he used at Philippi, hopping forty paces in a public street, she remains an enchantress. Her spirit is made of wind and flame, and the poet in him worships her no less than the man. He is under no illusion about her, knows all her faults, sees through her wiles, believes her capable of betraying him. It makes no difference. She is his heart's desire made perfect. To love her is what he was born for. What have the gods in heaven to say against it? To imagine heaven is to imagine her; to die is to rejoin her. To deny that this was love is the madness of morality. He gives her every atom of his heart.

She destroys him. Shakespeare, availing himself of the historic fact, portrays, on Antony's return to her, the suddenness and the depth of his descent. In spite of his own knowledge, the protests of his captains, the entreaties even of a private soldier, he fights by sea simply and solely because she wishes it. Then in mid-battle, when she flies, he deserts navy and army and his faithful thousands and follows her. 'I never saw an action of such shame,' cries Scarus; and we feel the dishonour of the hero keenly. Then Shakespeare begins to raise him again. First his own overwhelming sense of shame redeems him. Next, we watch the rage of the dying lion. Then the mere sally before the final defeat – a sally dismissed by Plutarch in three lines – is magnified into a battle, in which Antony displays to us, and himself feels for the last time, the glory of his soldiership. And, throughout, the magnanimity and gentleness which shine through his desperation endear him to us. How beautiful is his affection for his followers and even for his servants, and the devotion they return! How noble his reception of the news that Enobarbus has deserted him! How touchingly significant the refusal of Eros either to kill him or survive him! How pathetic and even sublime the completeness of his love for Cleopatra! His anger is born and dies in an hour. One tear, one kiss, outweighs his ruin. He believes she has sold him to his enemy, yet he kills himself because he hears that she is dead. When, dying, he learns that she has deceived him once more, no thought of reproach crosses his mind: he simply asks to be carried to her. He knows well that she is not capable of dying because he dies, but that does not sting him; when, in his last agony, he calls for wine that he may gain a moment's strength to speak, it is to advise her for the days to come. Shakespeare borrowed from Plutarch the final speech of Antony. It is fine, but it is not miraculous. The miraculous speeches belong only to his own hero:

> I am dying, Egypt, dying; only
> I here importune death awhile, until
> Of many thousand kisses the poor last
> I lay upon thy lips;

or the first words he utters when he hears of Cleopatra's death:

> Unarm, Eros; the long day's task is done,
> And we must sleep.

If he meant the task of statesman and warrior, that is not what his words mean to us.   (pp. 293–8) □

Cleopatra is described with as many exclamations of wonder as Antony but Bradley's interrogation of the tragedy is less penetrating as its end approaches. Before the last battle, Octavius had announced 'the time of universal peace is near', and yet, when that battle has been won and his soldiers take command of the stage, Bradley allows military and political issues to slip out of sight as he pays glowing tribute to the two ageing lovers and the transcendence of their forbidden love.

■ Many unpleasant things can be said of Cleopatra; and the more that are said the more wonderful she appears. The exercise of sexual attraction is the element of her life; and she has developed nature into a consummate art. When she cannot exert it on the present lover she imagines its effects on him in absence. Longing for the living, she remembers with pride and joy the dead; and the past which the furious Antony holds up to her as a picture of shame is, for her, glory. She cannot see an ambassador, scarcely even a messenger, without desiring to bewitch him. Her mind is saturated with this element. If she is dark, it is because the sun himself has been amorous of her. Even when death is close at hand she imagines his touch as a lover's. She embraces him that she may overtake Iras and gain Antony's first kiss in the other world. . . .

Some of her feelings are violent, and, unless for a purpose, she does not dream of restraining them; her sighs and tears are winds and waters, storms and tempests. At times, as when she threatens to give Charmian bloody teeth, or hales the luckless Messenger up and down by the hair, strikes him and draws her knife on him, she resembles (if I dare say it) Doll Tearsheet sublimated. She is a mother; but the threat of Octavius to destroy her children if she takes her own life passes by her like the wind (a point where Shakespeare contradicts Plutarch). She ruins a great man, but shows no sense of the tragedy of his ruin. The anguish of spirit that appears in his language to his servants is beyond her; she has to ask Enobarbus what he means. Can we feel sure that she would not have sacrificed him if she could have saved herself by doing so? It is not even certain that she did not attempt it. Antony himself believes that she did – that the fleet went over to Octavius by her orders. . . . She is willing also to survive her lover. Her first thought, to follow him after the high roman fashion, is too great for her. She would live on if she could, and would cheat her victor too of the best part of her fortune. The thing that drives her to die is the certainty that she will be carried to Rome to grace his triumph. That alone decides her. The marvellous thing is that the knowledge of all this makes hardly more difference to us than it did to Antony. . . .

That which makes her wonderful and sovereign laughs at definition, but she herself came nearest naming it when, in the final speech (a passage surpassed in poetry, if at all, only by the final speech of Othello), she cries,

I am fire and air; my other elements
I give to baser life.

The fire and air which at death break from union with those other elements, transfigured them during her life, and still convert into engines of enchantment the very things for which she is condemned. . . .

With all our admiration and sympathy for the lovers we do not wish them to gain the world. It is better for the world's sake, and not less for their own, that they should fail and die. At the very first they came before us . . . in a glory already tarnished, half-ruined by their past. Indeed one source of strange and most unusual effect in their story is that this marvellous passion comes to adepts in the experience and art of passion, who might be expected to have worn its charm away. Its splendour dazzles us; but, when the splendour vanishes, we do not mourn, as we mourn for the love of Romeo or Othello, that a thing so bright and good should die. And the fact that we mourn so little saddens us.   (pp. 300–4) □

CHAPTER THIRTEEN

Coriolanus

■ Most of the great tragedies leave a certain imaginative impression of the highest value . . . what we witness is not the passion and doom of mere individuals. The forces that meet in the tragedy stretch far beyond the little group of figures and the tiny tract of space and time in which they appear. The darkness that covers . . . the hero's fate is, in one sense, intelligible, for it follows from his character and the conditions in which he is placed; and yet everything, character, conditions, and issue, is mystery. Now of this effect there is very little in *Coriolanus*. No doubt the story has a universal meaning, since the contending forces are permanent constituents of human nature; but that peculiar *imaginative* effect of atmosphere is hardly felt. And, thinking of the play, we notice that the means by which it is produced elsewhere are almost absent here. One of these means is the use of the supernatural; another a treatment of nature which makes her appear not merely as a background, nor even merely as a conscious witness of human feelings, sufferings, and deeds, but as a vaster fellow actor and fellow-sufferer. Remove in fancy from *Hamlet*, *Lear*, and *Macbeth* all that appeals to imagination through these means, and you find them utterly changed, but brought nearer to *Coriolanus*. . . . [Its hero] was not the man to be terrified by twilight, or to feel that the stars or the wind took part against or with him. If Lear's thunderstorm had beat upon his head, he would merely have set his teeth. And not only is the mystery of nature absent; she is scarcely present even as a background. The hero's grim description of his abode in exile as 'the city of kites and crows' (it is not in [his source,] Plutarch), is almost all we have. In short, *Coriolanus* has scarcely more atmosphere, either supernatural or natural, than the average serious prose drama of to-day.

In Shakespeare's greatest tragedies there is a second source – in one or two the chief source – of supreme imaginative appeal, the exhibition of inward conflict, or of the outburst of one or another passion, terrible, heart-rending, or glorious to witness. At these moments the speaker becomes the greatest of poets; and yet, the dramatic convention admitted, he speaks in character. The hero in Coriolanus is never thus the greatest of poets, and he could not be so without a breach of more than dramatic convention. His nature is large, simple, passionate; but (except in one point, to which I will return, as it is irrelevant here) his nature is not, in any marked degree, imaginative. . . . He is very eloquent, but his only free eloquence is that of vituperation and scorn. It is sometimes more than eloquence, it is splendid poetry; but it is never such magical poetry as we hear in the four greatest tragedies. Then, too, it lies in his nature that his deepest and most sacred feeling, that for his mother, is almost dumb. It governs his life and leads him uncomplaining towards death, but it cannot speak. And, finally, his inward conflicts are veiled from us. The change that came when he found himself alone and homeless in exile is not exhibited. The result is partly seen in the one soliloquy of this drama, but the process is hidden. Of the passion that possesses him when his triumph seems at hand we get a far more vivid idea from the words of Cominius than from any words of his own:

> I tell you he does sit in gold, his eye
> Red as 'twould burn Rome.

In the most famous scene, when his fate is being decided, only one short sentence reveals the gradual loosening of his purpose during his mother's speech. The actor's face and hands and bearing must show it, not the hero's voice; and his submission is announced in a few quiet words, deeply moving and impressive, but destitute of the effect we know elsewhere of a lightning-flash that rends the darkness and discloses every cranny of the speaker's soul. All this we can see to be as it should be, but it does set limits to the flight of Shakespeare's imagination.   (pp. 75–8) □

Although Bradley believed that 'a political conflict is never the centre of interest in Shakespeare's plays', *he acknowledged that here it was* 'very prominent' (p. 79). *Nevertheless, after briefly recounting opinions on the matter that were then current and sidestepping the charge that Shakespeare himself* 'loathed the common Englishman', *he turned back to the tragedy to consider it in his usual terms, which were inherited from Aristotle, defining the conflict inherent in its action and the tragic flaw of its hero.*

■ The representation of the people [of Rome], whatever else it may be, is part of a dramatic design. This design is based on the main facts of the story, and these imply a certain character in the people and the hero. Since the issue is tragic, the conflict between them must be felt to be unavoidable and wellnigh hopeless. The necessity for dramatic sympathy with both sides demands that on both there should be some right and some wrong, both virtues and failings; and if the hero's monstrous purpose of destroying his native city is not to extinguish our sympathy, the provocation he receives must be great. This being so, the picture of the people is, surely, no darker than it had to be; the desired result would have been more easily secured by making it darker still. And one must go further . . . the conflict of hero and people is hopeless; but it is he alone who makes the conflict of patricians and plebeians . . . in any high degree dangerous.

The people have bad faults, but no such faults as, in his absence, would prevent a constitutional development in their favour. . . . When the arts of the tribunes have provoked him to such a storm of defiant and revolutionary speech that both the consulship and his life are in danger, one feels that another man might save both with no great trouble. Menenius tells him that the people

> have pardons, being ask'd, as free
> As words to little purpose.

His mother and friends urge him to deceive the people with false promises. But neither false promises nor apologies are needed, only a little humanity and some acknowledgement that the people are part of the state. He is capable of neither, and so the conflict is hopeless. But it is so not because the people, or even the tribunes, are what they are, but because he is what we call an 'impossible' person. The result is that all the force and nobility of Rome's greatest man have to be thrown away and wasted. That is tragic; and it is doubly so because it is not only his faults that make him impossible. There is bound up with them a nobleness of nature in which he surpasses every one around him.

We see this if we consider, what is not always clear to the reader, his political position. It is not shared by any of the other patricians who appear in the drama. Critics have called him a Tory or an ultra-Tory; but the tribune who calls him a 'traitorous innovator' is quite as near the mark. The people have been granted tribunes. The tribunate is a part of the constitution, and it is accepted, with whatever reluctance, by the other patricians. But Coriolanus would abolish it, and that not by law but by the sword. Nor would this content him. The right of the people to control the election of the consul is no new thing; it is an old traditional right; but it too, he says, might well be taken away. The only constitution tolerable in his eyes is one where the patricians are the state, and the people a mere instrument to feed it and fight for it. It is this conviction that makes it so dangerous to appoint him consul, and also makes it impossible for him to give way. Even if he could ask pardon for his abuse of the people, he could not honestly promise to acknowledge their political rights.

Now the nobleness of his nature is at work here. He is not tyrannical; the charge brought against him of aiming at a tyranny is silly. ... Shakespeare's hero, though he feels his superiority to his fellow patricians, always treats them as equals. He is never rude or over-bearing. He speaks to them with the simple directness or the bluff familiarity of a comrade. He does not resent their advice, criticism, or reproof. He shows no trace of envy or jealousy, or even of satisfaction at having surpassed them. ... The patricians are his fellows in a community of virtue – of a courage, fidelity, and honour . . . [and] the bright ideal of such virtue become perfect still urges them on. But the plebeians, in his eyes, are destitute of this virtue, and therefore have no place in this community. All they care for is food in peace, looting in war, flattery from their demagogues; and they will not even clean their teeth. To ask anything of them is to insult not merely himself but the virtues that he worships. To give them a real share in citizenship is treason to Rome; for Rome means these virtues. They are not Romans, they are the rats of Rome.

He is very unjust to them, and his ideal, though high, is also narrow. But he is magnificently true to it, and even when he most repels us we feel this and glory in him. He is never more true to it than when he tries to be false; and this is the scene where his superiority in nobleness is most apparent. He, who had said of his enemy, 'I hate him worse than a promise-breaker,' is urged to save himself and his friends by promises that he means to break. To his mother's argument that he ought no more to mind deceiving the people than outwitting an enemy in war, he cannot give the obvious answer, for he does not really count the people his fellow-countrymen; but the proposal that *he* should descend to lying or flattering astounds him. He feels that if he does so he will never be himself again; that his mind will have taken on an inherent baseness and no mere simulated one. And he is sure, as we are, that he simply cannot do what is required of him. When at last he consents to try, it is solely because his mother bids him and he cannot resist her chiding. Often he reminds us of a huge boy; and here he acts like a boy whose sense of honour is finer than his mother's, but who is too simple and too noble to frame the thought.

Unfortunately he is altogether too simple and too ignorant of himself. Though he is the proudest man in Shakespeare he seems to be unaware of his pride, and is hurt when his mother mentions it. It does not prevent him from being genuinely modest, for he never dreams that he has attained the ideal he worships; yet the sense of his own

greatness is twisted round every strand of this worship. In almost all
his words and deeds we are conscious of the tangle. I take a single
illustration. He cannot endure to be praised. Even his mother, who has
a charter to extol her blood, grieves him when she praises him. As for
others,

> I had rather have one scratch my head i' the sun
> When the alarum were struck, than idly sit
> To hear my nothings monster'd.

His answer to the roar of the army hailing him 'Coriolanus' is, 'I will
go wash.' His wounds are 'scratches with briars'. In Plutarch he shows
them to the people without demur; in Shakespeare he would rather
lose the consulship. There is a greatness in all this that makes us exult.
But who can assign the proportions of the elements that compose this
impatience of praise: the feeling (which we are surprised to hear him
express) that he, like hundreds more, has simply done what he could;
the sense that it is nothihg to what might be done; the want of human
sympathy; . . . the pride which makes him feel that he needs no recognition, that after all he himself could do ten times as much, and that
to praise his achievement implies a limit to his power? If any one could
solve this problem, Coriolanus certainly could not. To adapt a phrase
in the play, he has no more introspection in him than a tiger. So he
thinks that his loathing of the people is all disgust at worthlessness, and
his resentment in exile all a just indignation. So too he fancies that he
can stand

> As if a man were author of himself
> And knew no other kin,

while in fact public honour and home affections are the breath of his
nostrils, and there is not a drop of stoic blood in his veins.

What follows on his exile depends on this self-ignorance. When he
bids farewell to his mother and wife and friends he is still excited and
exalted by conflict. He comforts them; he will take no companion; he
will be loved when he is lacked, or at least he will be feared; while he
remains alive, they shall always hear from him, and never aught but
what is like him formerly. But the days go by, and no one, not even
his mother, hears a word. When we see him next, he is entering
Antium to offer his services against his country. If they are accepted,
he knows what he will do; he will burn Rome.

. . . Shakespeare does not exhibit to us the change of mind which
issues in this frightful purpose; but . . . gradually the blind intolerable
chaos of resentment conceives and gives birth to a vision, not merely

155

of battle and indiscriminate slaughter, but of the whole city one tower of flame. To see that with his bodily eyes would satisfy his soul; and the way to the sight is through the Volscians. If he is killed the moment they recognize him, he cares little; better a dead nothing than the living nothing Rome thinks him. But if he lives, she shall know what he is. He bears himself among the Volscians with something that resembles self-control; but what controls him is the vision that never leaves him and never changes, and his eye is red with its glare when he sits in his state before the doomed city.

This is Shakespeare's idea, not Plutarch's. In Plutarch there is not a syllable about the burning of Rome. Coriolanus (to simplify a complicated story) intends to humiliate his country by forcing on it disgraceful terms of peace. . . . What Shakespeare wanted was a simpler and more appalling situation than he found in Plutarch, and a hero enslaved by his passion and driven blindly forward . . . a man totally ignorant of himself, and stumbling to the destruction either of his life or of his soul. . . . The famous scene where he is confronted with Volumnia and Valeria, Virgilia and her boy, and the issue is decided . . . is one in which the tragic feelings of fear and pity have little place. Such anxiety as I feel is not for the fate of the hero or of any one else; it is, to use religious language, for the safety of his soul. And when he yields, though I know, as he divines, that his life is lost, the emotion I feel is not pity; he is above pity and above life. And the anxiety itself is but slight: it bears no resemblance to the hopes and fears that agitate us as we approach the end in *Othello* or *King Lear*. The whole scene affects me, to exaggerate a little, more as a majestic picture of stationary figures than as the fateful climax of an action speeding to its close. And the structure of the drama seems to confirm this view.

Almost throughout the first three Acts – that is, up to the banishment – we have incessant motion, excited and resounding speech, a violent oscillation of fortunes. But, after this, the dramatic tension is suddenly relaxed, and, though it increases again, it is never allowed to approach its previous height. . . . From the moment when he catches sight of the advancing figures, and the voice of nature – what he himself calls 'great nature' – begins to speak in his heart long before it speaks aloud to his ear, we know the end. And all this is in harmony with that characteristic of the drama which we noticed at first – we feel but faintly, if at all, the presence of any mysterious or fateful agency. We are witnessing only the conquest of passion by simple human feelings, and *Coriolanus* is as much a drama of reconciliation as a tragedy. That is no defect in it, but it is a reason why it cannot leave the same impression as the supreme tragedies, and should be judged by its own standards.

A tragedy it is, for the passion is gigantic, and it leads to the hero's death. But the catastrophe scarcely diminishes the influence of the great scene. Since we know that his nature, though the good in it has conquered, remains unchanged, and since his rival's plan is concerted before our eyes, we wait with little suspense, almost indeed with tranquillity, the certain end. As it approaches it is felt to be the more inevitable because the steps which lead to it are made to repeat as exactly as possible the steps which led to his exile. His task, as then, is to excuse himself, a task the most repugnant to his pride. Aufidius, like the tribunes then, knows how to render its fulfilment impossible. He hears a word of insult, the same that he heard then – 'traitor'. It is followed by a sneer at the most sacred tears he ever shed, and a lying description of their effect on the bystanders; and his pride, and his loathing of falsehood and meanness, explode, as before, in furious speech. For a moment he tries to check himself and appeals to the senators; but the effort seems only to treble his rage. Though no man, since Aufidius spoke, has said a word against him, he defies the whole nation, recalling the day of its shame and his own triumph, when alone, like an eagle, he fluttered the dovecotes in Corioli. The people, who had accompanied him to the market-place, splitting the air with the noise of their enthusiasm, remember their kinsfolk whom he slaughtered, change sides, and clamour for his death. As he turns on Aufidius, the conspirators rush upon him, and in a moment, before the vision of his glory has faded from his brain, he lies dead. The instantaneous cessation of enormous energy (which is like nothing else in Shakespeare) strikes us with awe, but not with pity. As I said, the effect of the preceding scene, where he conquered something stronger than all the Volscians and escaped something worse than death, is not reversed; it is only heightened by a renewed joy in his greatness. Roman and Volscian will have peace now, and in his native city patrician and plebeian will move along the way he barred. And they are in life, and he is not. But life has suddenly shrunk and dwindled, and become a home for pygmies and not for him.   (pp. 81–95) □

Having shown that Coriolanus *is not confined by his idea of what constituted a* 'Shakespearean Tragedy' *or a tragic hero, Bradley turns to a discussion of its characters to point out other differences, first noting an unusually widespread humour:*

■ When the people [i.e., *plebeians*] appear as individuals they are frequently more or less comical. . . . The talk of the servants with one another and with the muffled hero and the conversation of the sentinels with Menenius, are amusing. There is a touch of comedy in the contrast between Volumnia and Virgilia when we see them on occasions not too serious. And then, not only at the beginning, as in Plutarch, but throughout the story we meet with that pleasant and wise old gentleman Menenius, whose humour tells him how to keep the peace while he gains his point, and to say without offence what the hero cannot say without raising a storm. Perhaps no one else in the play is regarded from beginning to end with such unmingled approval, and this is not lessened when the failure of his embassy to Coriolanus makes him the subject as well as the author of mirth. If we regard the drama from this point of view we find that it differs from almost all the tragedies, though it has a certain likeness of *Antony and Cleopatra*. What is amusing in it is, for the most part, simply amusing, and has no tragic tinge. It is not like the gibes of Hamlet at Polonius, or the jokes of the clown who . . . is digging Ophelia's grave, or that humour of Iago which for us is full of menace; and who could dream of comparing it with the jesting of Lear's fool? Even that Shakespearean audacity, the interruption of Volumnia's speech by the hero's little son, makes one laugh almost without reserve. And all this helps to produce the characteristic tone of this tragedy.   (pp. 96–7) □

The character of Aufidius is quickly (and strangely) dismissed as 'by far the weakest spot in the drama' but when Bradley turns to Volumnia and Virgilia he marks another significant difference from other tragedies in that, at the end, these characters depend not only on the words they speak but also, significantly, on the quality of performance when words cease.

■ Though this play is by no means a drama of destiny we might almost say that Volumnia is responsible for the hero's life and death. She trained him from the first to aim at honour in arms, to despise pain, and to

> forget that ever
> He heard the name of death;

to strive constantly to surpass himself, and to regard the populace with inhuman disdain as

> things created
> To buy and sell with groats.

Thus she led him to glory and to banishment. And it was she who, in the hour of trial, brought him to sacrifice his pride and his life.

Her sense of personal honour, we saw, was less keen than his; but she was much more patriotic. We feel this superiority even in the scene that reveals the defect; in her last scene we feel it alone. She has idolized her son; but, whatever motive she may appeal to in her effort to move him, it is not of him she thinks; her eyes look past him and are set on Rome. When, in yielding, he tells her that she has won a happy victory for her country, but a victory most dangerous, if not most mortal, to her son, she answers nothing. And her silence is sublime.

These last words would be true of Plutarch's Volumnia. But in Plutarch, though we hear of the son's devotion, and how he did great deeds to delight his mother, neither his early passion for war nor his attitude to the people is attributed to her influence, and she has no place in the action until she goes to plead with him. Hence she appears only in majesty, while Shakespeare's Volumnia has a more varied part to play. She cannot be majestic when we see her hurrying through the streets in wild exultation at the news of his triumph; and where, angrily conquering her tears, she rails at the authors of his banishment. . . . What Shakespeare gains by her animation and vehemence in these scenes is not confined to them. He prepares for the final scene a sense of contrast which makes it doubly moving and impressive.

In Volumnia's great speech he is much indebted to Plutarch, and it is, on the whole, in the majestic parts that he keeps most close to his authority. The open appeal to affection is his own; and so are the touches of familiar language. It is his Volumnia who exclaims, 'here he lets me prate like one i' the stocks', and who compares herself, as she once was, to a hen that clucks her chickens home. But then the conclusion, too, is pure Shakespeare; and if it has not majesty it has something dramatically even more potent. Volumnia, abandoning or feigning to abandon hope, turns to her companions with the words:

> Come, let us go;
> This fellow had a Volscian to his mother;
> His wife is in Corioli, and his child
> Like him by chance. Yet give us our despatch:
> I am hush'd until our city be a-fire,
> And then I'll speak a little.

Her son's resolution has long been tottering, but now it falls at once. Throughout, it is not the substance of her appeals that moves him, but the bare fact that she appeals, and the culmination is that she ceases to appeal, and defies him. . . . On a lower level exactly the same thing happens when she tries to persuade him to go and deceive the people. The moment she stops, and says, in effect, 'Well, then, follow your own will,' his will gives way. Deliberately to set it against hers is beyond his power.

[To call Virgilia 'lovely' and 'submissive'] can hardly be the whole truth about a woman who inflexibly rejects the repeated invitations of her formidable mother-in-law and her charming friend [Valeria] to leave the house; who later does what she can to rival Volumnia in rating the tribunes; and who at last quietly seconds Volumnia's assurance that Coriolanus shall only enter Rome over her body. . . . The indefinable impression which . . . thousands of readers share . . . comes in part from that kind of muteness in which Virgilia resembles Cordelia, and which is made to suggest a world of feeling in reserve. And in part it comes from the words of her husband. His greeting when he returns from the war, and she stands speechless before him:

> My gracious silence, hail!
> Wouldst thou have laugh'd had I come coffin'd home,
> That weep'st to see me triumph? Ah, my dear,
> Such eyes the widows in Corioli wear,
> And mothers that lack sons:

his exclamation when he sees her approaching at their last meeting and speaks first of her and not of Volumnia:

> What is that curtsy worth, or those doves' eyes
> Which can make gods forsworn? I melt, and am not
> Of stronger earth than others;

these words envelope Virgilia in a radiance which is reflected back upon himself. And this is true also of his praise of Valeria in the lines perhaps most often quoted from this drama:

> The noble sister of Publicola,
> The moon of Rome, chaste as the icicle
> That's curdied by the frost from purest snow,
> And hangs on Dian's temple: dear Valeria!

I said that at one point the hero's nature *was* in a high degree imaginative; and it is here. In his huge violent heart there was a store, not only of tender affection, but of delicate and chivalrous poetry. And though Virgilia and Valeria evoke its expression we cannot limit its range: it extends to the widows and mothers in Corioli. . . .   (pp. 98–102) □

Biographical notes

on persons mentioned in the lectures

Coleridge, Samuel Taylor (1772–1834), poet and critic. His Shakespeare criticism was published in *Biographia Literaria* (1817) and *Notes and Lectures upon Shakespeare* (1849). S. T. Coleridge, *Lectures 1808–1819: On Literature* (Princeton, NJ: Princeton University Press, 1987) is the most reliable edition.

Empedocles (*fl. c.* 444 BC), Sicilian philosopher who argued that the forces of love and hate governed the world.

Goethe, Johann Wolfgang von (1749–1832), poet, critic, playwright, theatre director. Among his many references to Shakespeare, the most famous is the analysis of Hamlet's character in *Wilhelm Meister* (1795).

Hazlitt, William (1778–1830), writer and critic. His most influential Shakespeare criticism was published in *The Characters of Shakespeare's Plays* (1817) and has frequently been republished.

Johnson, Samuel (1709–84), writer and critic. The Preface to his edition of Shakespeare (1765) was remarkable for its account of faults as well as excellencies.

Salvini, Tommaso (1829–1912), Italian tragic actor. He performed his most famous role, Othello, in England and America.

Schlegel, August Wilhelm von (1767–1845), translator and critic. His translations of sixteen of Shakespeare's plays were published in 1797–1801; his lectures *On Dramatic Art and Literature* were given in Vienna in 1808 and published in 1809–11.

Siddons, Sarah (1755–1831), actress. Her most famous part was Lady Macbeth, first performed in 1785. She retired from the stage in 1819.

Swinburne, Algernon Charles (1837–1909), poet and critic. *A Study of Shakespeare* (1880) followed essays and studies on Ben Jonson, George Chapman and other Elizabethans.

Tree, Beerbohm (1853–1917), actor and theatre manager. His spectacular productions included *Macbeth* and *Othello*.

Index
to authors, other than
Shakespeare